DATE DUE

DEMCO 38-297

Let The Righteous Speak!

Travel Memoirs

by CLEMONCE SABOURIN

PAGEANT PRESS, INC.
NEW YORK

▲

TO MY WIFE

Perhaps in heaven, darling,
there will be no need to speak
of race • • •

This is the raw material of sociology, the human sore
to which the balm of the Word—
preached and practiced—must be applied.

C.S.

IT BEGAN WHEN SOMEONE SPOKE OF THE ENCHANTMENT OF gliding in a glass-bottomed boat over the placid waters of Silver Springs in Florida. That was in December. When July rolled around we packed the car and headed South. Our first stop was to be Petersburg, Virginia.

This stretch is routine for us, for Petersburg is my wife's home, and we drive down at least once a year. She and Clemmie, our son, generally spend July and August there.

Ten years ago, going down by Route One, it was not always pleasant. But today we take the Jersey Turnpike and turn in for gas and refreshments at the last Howard Johnson's. This enables us to cover the remaining two hundred sixty-two miles, by way of the Delaware Memorial and Chesapeake Bay bridges, without the strain of fatigue, hunger, or the necessity of using rest rooms. Thus, the new roads and bridges which permit us to bypass Trenton, Philadelphia, Baltimore, Washington, Alexandria, and Fredericksburg, have been a special boon to the Sabourins. The only large city we have to contend with is Richmond, but that we can take in good spirit, for once through Richmond, we have only twenty miles to go.

Petersburg, population 35,000, manufactures tobacco products, textiles, trunks and luggage, leather goods, and optical instruments. On one side of the city is the State College for Negroes, and on the other, the State Hospital for the Negro insane. A local character told me, tongue in cheek, that some of the best citizens are graduates of both.

1

One of our vacation problems (encountered my first July in Petersburg) was finding a place to worship. The most convenient thing would have been to attend a church of our own synod, some twenty miles away. But I was afraid to take that risk. Later, in another city, I met the pastor of that church and said, "Oh, yes, I know where your church is. I usually spend the month of July in Petersburg, and last summer I was told about your place after my wife and I had driven a hundred miles farther on to attend services in Washington." This was met with an embarrassing silence. So . . . we talked of something else . . .

Some years later, my wife's brother, a brick mason by trade, told me that his company had just completed a new Lutheran church. He wanted me to see it.

We drove into a section where scores of new cottages sat back on spacious lawns. Many homes were still under construction. Soon the church loomed up, as pretty as a picture. We drew up to the curb, got out, and slowly circled the building, my brother-in-law pointing out details of construction.

Before we reached our car, a Chevvy pulled up. A portly, red-faced man got out and walked toward the door.

"We were just admiring your new building," I said. "How old is your congregation?"

I introduced myself and said a few words about our work in Manhattan. I told him that my wife and I usually spend our vacation in Petersburg.

Once he opened up, he was quite enthusiastic. It was a United Lutheran Church congregation. He was an officer. He had come a little early to open up for a meeting. He beamed as we spoke of the beauty of the new building. But, although he had the keys in his hand and in spite of his evi-

2

dent pride over the beauty of the place, he did not offer to show us how it looked on the inside. . . .

So, when we want to worship in Petersburg, we attend the Baptist church in which my wife was reared. It is a big church, an old church. And the services are so dry and formal and painfully correct, that after the first drowsy nod I feel as though I am worshiping in my own congregation.

It was in Petersburg that we began having trouble with Clemmie. If only Negro children were delivered with an innate knowledge of their "proper place" in the Southern white man's scheme of things, it would certainly make matters easier for their parents!

There is a playground just across the street from my wife's home. Several years ago, the first year it was equipped and opened to the children of the community, Clemmie and I were sitting on the porch watching the children under the sprinkler. After awhile, Clemmie said, "Daddy, I want to get wet."

"No, you have no bathing suit."

"Daddy, I want to go swing."

"No, you are in a swing now, right on your own porch."

"Daddy, can I play ball with those boys?"

"No, Clemmie. You are too small!"

Negro and white children ride their bikes together up and down the length of Shepherd Street. They play together in back yards, on front porches, on the sidewalks and in the street. But step off the sidewalk, and over the invisible line that marks the boundary of this community playground, and the games become "white only." It goes without saying that the adult Christians were the ones who laid down the rules.

One day last summer, as I watched the boys in the "white-only" park, the first baseman made a terrific play and a yell went up from the "white-only" sideline—"Ol' Jackie Robinson!"

After awhile a little fellow hit a long one and circled the bases. As soon as he had caught enough breath for the purpose, he shouted, "Man, I'm Roy Campanella!"

The strange thing was that when Campanella smacked his homer Don Newcombe was pitching.

That summer I took Clemmie downtown only once. That once was enough for me.

In a crowded section of the little business district he grabbed my hand and, pulling me to a stop, said, "Look, Daddy! Hoppy! Come on, Daddy, let's go see Hoppy!"

"No, Clemmie. You have seen enough of Hoppy already."

A few blocks farther on the same thing happened. This time it was Gene Autry.

"Clemmie, we don't have time."

"But, Daddy, you never have time to take me to the movies at home. What do you have to do now?"

"Come on. Let's go!"

Later we turned into a drugstore to pick up a magazine. Several children about Clemmie's age were sitting at the soda fountain.

"Daddy, let's get a soda. I want a soda, Daddy!"

"Come on, Clemmie. We are going home. Mamma is waiting for us."

"But, Daddy!"

"COME ON, Clemmie!"

But why should I get angry with him? How could he know unless someone tells him? And how can one tell him without planting in his heart a seed of hatred against those who are responsible for this?

Many of my well-meaning friends counsel patience.

4

"Things are improving. Twenty years from now it will be quite different."

Yes, but twenty years from now Clemmie will have lost the capacity to enjoy these simple childhood delights. Twenty years from now he may be lying on some God-forsaken battlefield coughing out his life . . . dying for the very people who would not permit him to live like a human being.

Nowhere in the South can one avoid a discussion of the race problem. This is especially true among the Negroes. Petersburg is not in the deep South, but even here it strikes you full force. And the pattern it follows is typical of the entire South.

The whites argue that Negro children cannot be permitted to attend school with white children because of the low I.Q. of many of the Negro children, because of their high disease rate, and because of their high rate of illegitimacy.

Negroes counter: that if the first two of these propositions are true, then perhaps the answer is segregation, but not segregation based on race. Rather, place dumb Negro children with dumb white children and diseased Negro children with diseased white children. As to the high rate of illegitimacy among Negro children, that could be met by finding an answer to the question: "Who or what is a Negro,"; by better job opportunities for Negroes, and by a general overhauling of marriage laws, especially the one against intermarriage, a law which, for generations has been interpreted by predatory white men as an invitation to open season on Negro women.

The whites argue further that they simply cannot place their children in the hands of Negro teachers. The peculiar thing about this determination is that traditionally, every white family that could scrape up an extra three, five, or seven dollars a week, hired Negro women, at times illiterate, to wash the clothes they wore, cook the food they ate, and take care of the children they bore—and that during the most formative period of their lives. Even today it is not uncommon to hear a prominent white man say, in proof of his love for Negroes—*in their place*—that he was brought up by a dear old Negro Mammy.

The fact of the matter is that many white children might be better off in the hands of Negro teachers. In North Carolina I was told that statewise the Negro teachers have a higher degree of professional training than the whites. While this may not be true of the entire state of Virginia, it is true in certain sections.

For many years the only decent job opportunities open to Negroes were in the teaching profession. Many Negro men prepared to make this their life's work. Negro women sought teaching positions, not as a stopgap between school and marriage, but as lifetime careers. Because Southern universities would not accept them, and because Negro colleges could not offer them advanced degrees, they were forced to seek further training elsewhere. Thus, by force of circumstance, many Negro teachers in the South are graduates of the best universities in the country. Of course, to quote a Maryland school official in reply to these facts, "White teachers do not need advanced training. Their cultural background makes them better teachers than the Negroes." It is reliably reported that that's what the man said.

Be it said in all honesty that not all of the white people of the South are against integration. There are some strong voices in favor of it.

Among the Negroes there is more unanimity. In spite of

the fact that integration threatens the position of the Negro teacher, (and he is constantly reminded of it), I have yet to talk to a single Negro teacher who is not in favor of integration. And among the Negroes in general, whenever you find a person who speaks against integration, you can bet that either he has built up a strong retaliatory hatred against white people, or that he is afraid.

In one respect all the Negroes of the South are afraid, even the most aggressive. Yes, they are afraid of the thing they have to do. But for the sake of their children, for the sake of generations yet unborn, and for the sake of saving their country from its own undoing, they are determined to do it.

In Petersburg, thirty-two Negroes signed a petition contending that they were unlawfully denied the use of Wilcox Lake, a municipal facility. Among those who signed was Alfonso McCain, executive in charge of the Negro "Y." McCain was fired!

The term "Economic Sanction" is becoming painfully familiar to the Negroes of the South. Its intensified use is causing genuine hardship. But it does not stop there. When to economic sanction you add the destruction of Negro homes and the shotgunning of Negro leaders, you get a picture quite reminiscent of Hitler's pogrom against the Jews.

My wife's sister, Ruby, is principal of a fifteen-teacher elementary school. She is a good driver and good company. We were anxious to have her accompany us on our trip, and for that reason spent several days waiting for her to wind up her year-end work at the school.

I had taken some tools down so that I could spend the time making a few repairs around the place. When the repairs were completed, I made a front-seat carrier for our water jug, drinking glasses and lunch. It turned out to be such a convenient gadget that my wife still wants me to patent it and put it on the market.

Ruby and I decided that we would drive in two-hour shifts so that it would not become burdensome to either of us. But I am sure that by the time the trip was over she had spent more hours behind the wheel than I. I can take it or leave it. She loves it . . .

The stretch from Petersburg, Virginia to Winston-Salem, North Carolina, like that from New York to Petersburg, is old hat to us. In Winston-Salem, too, my wife has a sister. Elva is head of the English Department at Teacher's College and though, like Ruby, unmarried, she has a home on a hillside right where the city begins.

On one highway in Virginia we saw giant road machinery moving like a herd of prehistoric animals. Some were driven by Negroes, other by white men. Integration. . . . During my years in the South, whenever someone invented a machine to take the sweat out of a piece of work, it became a white man's job.

About an hour and a half after a brief stop at a roadside picnic table we slid past the Flamingo, made a sharp left, and drew up before the long concrete steps that lead up to Elva's house.

When we were here two years ago I drove Elva and Clemmie to the shopping district and left them there. Later that afternoon Elva came in, looking as though she had been squeezed through an emotional wringer.

She and Clemmie had boarded a bus to return home. Clemmie wanted to sit in the empty seat behind the driver. Elva said, "No, Clemmie, we can't sit here."

"But the seat is empty!" Even at seven Clemmie could argue like a Philadelphia lawyer.

8

"Clemmie, we are going to sit in the back."

"But, Aunt . . ."

"Come on, Clemmie!" And she took him by the hand and pulled him down the aisle.

A few stops later a white boy got on. He was just about Clemmie's age. He said to his mother, "Let's sit by the driver," and slid into the front seat.

Clemmie was all eyes. He yelled, "Look, Aunt Poppy," (his special name for Elva), "that boy is sitting by the driver."

"Yes, Clemmie, but he is white."

Holding his arms and hands before his eyes, as if to reassure himself, he blurted, "I am as white as he is!"

"Shut up, Clemmie!"

We used to sit on the front porch, watching the headlights turn in to the Flamingo, the drive-in theater just across the way, and Clemmie often asked us to take him there. He didn't mention it last summer. I think he is convinced that we simply don't like drive-in theaters.

Our stay was short, and Elva had a lot to say. Late into the night, it was schools and integration, and integration and schools, and much, much more of the same . . .

There are some fine Negro schools in North Carolina. In fact, in some places, I was told, they are better than the schools for the whites.

In North Carolina, probably the finest state in the South, the government officials tried to build a dam before the coming of the flood. Hoping that when the matter of segregated schools finally reached the Supreme Court, the Court would reaffirm its doctrine of separate but equal facilities, the state began to race against time. Millions were poured into Negro schools and colleges. . . . But it was too little, too late. A new day had dawned.

9

Next morning we were off. A new bypass enabled us to skirt Concord, the little town where I once taught school. We had to go through Charlotte, but not in a congested area. Here my wife once taught high-school home economics . . . and I served three years in the ministry. But we did not know each other then. . . . Gastonia, King's Mountain, and then the sign said: "Spartanburg, South Carolina."

"Is Spartanburg a large place?" Ruby asked.

"Good size," I muttered.

"Will we pass through the city?"

"Not if I can help it. I mean, yes, unless things have changed. But there is nothing there worth seeing."

A half hour later I was glad that I had said that, because a bypass loomed ahead.

"Let's take the bypass!"

The bypass was broad and smooth and almost traffic-free. See . . . the last time I arrived in Spartanburg it was midnight. I was spirited from a dingy bus station to a hiding place. The next night I stood three times under the glaring lights of a police line-up and was "identified" by two teen-age white girls, whom I have not seen to this day, as being the Negro who, from a distance of one hundred yards, across the bramble bush beside a railroad track, made indecent gestures at them. . . . Yes, there was nothing to see in Spartanburg . . . nothing I wanted to see.

It was a big filling station, the kind we were looking for. When we stopped at the pump I asked at attendant, "May we use your rest rooms?"

"Yes, right around the side."

When I came out I said, "Fill it up and check the oil." Then I told the others in the car that the place wasn't bad.

This became standard procedure. Where we could not use the rest rooms we would not buy gas.

I always went first. In some places the rest room marked "Colored" was so nasty and dirty that I would come out, tell the attendant to give me a few gallons, and then drive on.

A number of times we pulled into stations, saw a "White only" sign on an attached lunchroom, and then pulled away. Of course, this left us very uncomfortable at times. I soon understood the significance of the lunch box, water jug, and roll of toilet paper I once saw in the trunk of a Negro pastor's car.

We tried to be careful. My brother-in-law drove this route once. He stopped at night to get gas, and finding no one at the pump, he walked into the lunchroom. The man behind the counter yelled, "What do you want in here."

"I need some gas and I thought . . ."

"You know damned well you can't come in here!"

As the men at the counter sat glowering, the counterman shoved Jerry toward the back door and pushed him out.

Jerry was alone . . . and common sense prevailed.

But what if this happened to a man before his wife and child? Could he take it, or would he feel that it was better to die then and there?

No, I did not want to take that chance. It was this line of reasoning that led me, while I worked in the South, to travel alone. My wife never accompanied me anywhere unless I had previously been there and found the atmosphere to be fairly congenial. And although it is more than ten years since we left the South, the habit remains. No doubt that is why, when we got to the point at which we had to slacken our pace in New York City, we discovered that we had, quite unintentionally, developed a program that keeps either me or my wife on the job. The result is that occasionally,

11

when we want to go out together, we find it difficult to arrange.

We got the impression that the South is our new frontier —an industrial frontier. Everywhere we found cities and towns bursting at the seams, local industries expanding, and Northern industries seeking broad acres and cheap labor.

There is feverish religious activity also. There are new churches, old churches, big churches, little churches, churches that are khaki-colored tents by the side of the road. In old towns and cities, modernistic buildings stood like country cousins in their Sunday best, and not far away there was always the traditional church, standing with the grace and dignity that comes with age . . .

The churches advertise. In places the signs were so close together they looked like Burma Shave slogans. The farther South you go the thicker they get: "Jesus Saves," "Christ is the Answer," "Go to Church."

With all of these evidences of godliness about us, we felt like saying, "Surely this is the house of God; this is the gate to heaven."

We had just run a gauntlet of Gospel signs and crossed the city limits. This was Athens. The radio was low, but the voice was clear and distinct. In substance, it said this: "The Georgia Board of Education announced today that any teacher, Negro or white, found holding membership in the National Association for the Advancement of Colored People or otherwise supporting this organization, will be penalized. And any teacher, Negro or white, found teaching an integrated class will lose his license forever."

Ruby quickly added, ". . . and ever. Amen."

There are many fine homes in the South. And the grounds are beautiful. Driving into Atlanta is breathtaking. Goggle-eyed over a carpet of green that sloped down a terrace and

12

came to rest against the sidewalk, my wife exclaimed, "It looks manicured!" It was . . . Half a block further we saw an old Negro on his hands and knees clipping the hangnails . . .

This points up another question that haunts the Southern whites: If they give Negroes equal opportunities, what is going to become of the cheap servant class?

After stopping twice to ask directions, we found it—the University Motel.

We asked the manager whether there were a Negro hotel or motel in Montgomery. "No," he replied, "not that I know of. At least, nothing that I would recommend. Of course, you can always find a flea bag. . . . There is a nice place in Birmingham." He handed me a folder. . . . But we did not want to go to Birmingham . . .

The next morning when we went out to pack the car we noticed that just behind the two rows that made up the motel there was a large warehouse or factory. On either side there were dilapidated buildings, and across the bustling highway, hovels. The motel was attractive, even on the outside. It would have been beautiful if the owners had had any choice of location. But, still, it had an advantage. It was in town.

A short, stout man was at the ice machine filling his jug. He had been to Mississippi and was returning to Washington. I asked him about the possibility of finding decent quarters in Montgomery. "No," he said, "not there. Try Dorothy Hall at Tuskegee. It's about forty miles nearer than Montgomery. Your next day's drive will be that much longer. But you won't mind it after a good night's rest."

We were told that there was a Negro restaurant about one mile from the motel. The breakfast was ample. The waitress packed our lunch. We drove by and looked at the buildings of Atlanta University, then headed for Stone Mountain.

It was a very clear day, but even through our strong binoculars, this Confederate memorial, magnificent in conception, looked like a job just begun. When I flew over this monument several years ago, the glimpse I caught from the plane was more impressive. That was what brought me back . . .

Clemmie and I went into the souvenir shack. The middle-aged, female attendant was quite courteous. When we returned to our car, a white party had drawn up behind us. A smiling, mixed-gray man yelled as he walked toward us, "What part of the Bronx are you from?"

I answered, "I'm from Manhattan. I bought my tag in the Bronx."

He had been reared in New York but had settled in Georgia for business reasons. He seemed to be glad to see someone from home.

The next thing we wanted to see in Atlanta was the Wrenn, the home of Joel Chandler Harris, of Uncle Remus fame. We knew that many Negroes protest the Uncle Remus tales as being derogatory to the race. But after all, they are part of our literary history. It is quite possible that the Uncle Remus tales, like Aesop's fables, will live long after the last prejudiced American has choked to death on his own spittle.

It was not easy finding the place. Many we asked seemed never to have heard of it. But we had a street name and a house number, so we were steered nearer and nearer. We stopped at a filling station near a new Lutheran Church. The bulletin board said: "Frank C. Jones, Jr., Pastor." Going back, it would be on the right-hand side next to the big West End Baptist Church.

We had to park half a block away. I got out and walked

back alone. It was a large, low, dull-gray cottage, sitting back on a dreary-looking yard cluttered with trees. Near the front there was a sign bearing a picture of Uncle Remus. Before him, in rapt attention, sat a little blonde-haired girl. My mental summary was: quiet, dreary, a thing from days gone by . . . but not forbidding.

"Well, it is open to the public," I said, as I opened the door of the car. "Let's go in."

As we moved slowly over the uneven brick walk, a woman cracked the screen door and said, "Come right along. You are just in time for the story hour."

I felt better then. My few remaining fears vanished. We hesitated for a moment to look at a stone slab bearing the name of Margaret Mitchell, and then walked up the steps and across the porch.

The wrinkled white woman, wearing a wrinkled white dress, did a double take and began fumbling frantically with the latch. She tried to say something, but what we heard sounded like the clacking of loose-fitting dental plates. Finally she got out, "Where you all from?"

"New York!"

"Well, you see, we have never had any colored visitors."

"Does that mean that you can't have them?"

She ran back into the house and frantic but unintelligible voices poured out.

When she returned, visibly shaken, she said, "No, we just don't have any colored visitors."

"But your literature says that the Wrenn is open to the public. We came out of our way to see this place."

Turning on her heels behind the locked screen door, she threw back over her shoulder, "You'll just have to take it up with the authorities!"

Well, at least one Negro has been there—Uncle Remus. His shack is behind the big house . . .

There was not much conversation in our car as we pulled away—not even from Clemmie. And it was quite a while before even my over-cautious wife noticed that I was doing sixty in a thirty-mile zone . . .

When I think of the lush vegetation and pastoral beauty of the Alabama countryside it seems incongruous to speak of Tuskegee as an oasis. But in terms of human relations, that is what it is—an oasis.

Following the directions given us at the information stand, we pulled up to the curb at the Memorial, the famous statue of Booker T. Washington lifting the veil of ignorance from Negro youth. Dorothy Hall was opposite.

After we had checked in we walked half a block to the Carver Museum. As we made our way from exhibit to exhibit, we marveled at the evidence of this man's genius. What this slave-born scientist did to increase the wealth of an ungrateful South staggers the imagination!

When we got to Dr. Carver's original laboratory we saw a middle-aged white man holding the hand of a boy about ten. In subdued tones, with all the reverence of worship, he was telling the boy about Dr. Carver's hand-made equipment. When we passed, he nodded and smiled. Outside we saw them drive away in a car with an Alabama tag.

Hoping to see as much as we could before dark, we piled into the car and headed for the Veteran's Hospital. Near the dining hall, I stepped on the brake to ease the car over a road bump. As I rolled down the other side, someone yelled, "S-A-B-O-U-R-I-N!" On running feet, the voice materialized. It was Al Porter, principal of a school in North Carolina, now teaching summer classes at Tuskegee. He got in next to Clemmie and became our guide. We didn't know it before, but Porter had been brought up at Tuskegee. He knew it like a book. We saw not only the Veteran's Hospital, but almost everything else, including the site of Booker T. Washington's first chickencoop classroom.

That night, as we ate supper in the basement restaurant at Dorothy Hall, a young Negro woman came in. She was wearing a riding habit. With her was a young white man. They sat and had coffee and cake. They were still there when we left. No one seemed to notice their presence . . .

We were led to our second-floor quarters by way of pine-floored halls wide enough to drive a truck through. Broad, graceful arches reached from floor to ceiling. Soft lights, arched windows, and skillfully placed furniture, gave it the effect of a grand ballroom.

Our two enormous bedrooms were connected by a bath as large as many a New York kitchenette apartment. There were thermos pitchers of crushed ice on our marble-topped washstands. There were no air conditioners in the rooms. They were not needed. We didn't even plug in the electric fans we had brought along just in case. A quiet breeze rustled the leaves outside the windows. . . . We fell asleep in Dorothy Hall just a hundred yards from the chapel . . . and the graves of Booker T. Washington and George Washington Carver.

Next morning at breakfast, across from us sat Dr. Patterson, former Tuskegee President, now head of the Phelps Stokes Fund. Three white men sat eating breakfast and reading morning papers. But, as in the case of the couple we had seen the night before, no one paid any special attention to them. Their presence seemed to be the most natural thing in the world . . .

After the waitress had filled our jug and packed our food

17

for the day, we went out to the car. Porter was waiting. I told him that we had seen Dr. Patterson and then mentioned the perfectly casual way white people came into the place. His reply was, "Don't be surprised at that. Many of the wealthiest and most prominent people in the world have been guests at Dorothy Hall. The best hotels in the South cannot boast a finer clientele."

That morning we watched the workers in ceramics and then went from lab to lab in the Carver Foundation research building.

Our guide had a class coming up. He turned us down the right road and slid out the car.

"Thanks a million," I said. "We would not have seen half as much if we had not run into you. This place is wonderful. Here Southern Negroes walk with their shoulders back and their heads held high. Such a transformation . . ."

"Yes," said Porter, "but if you want to see a transformation that is absolutely ludicrous, you should see some of these same Negroes go to town and deal hat-in-hand with ignorant white men . . ."

There are still chain gangs in the South. Time and again we passed convicts working by the side of the road. And always, sitting on the side of a hill or under a nearby shade tree, there was a red-faced white man with a shotgun across his lap. One Negro told me that he did not consider it a disgrace to have been on a chain gang, because in Alabama a Negro may land on the chain gang for almost any reason imaginable. It could be, for instance, that you are just too familiar with a white man's Negro girl friend; for a white man simply will not tolerate his Negro girl friend's going out with Negro men, that is, unless she is pregnant. Of

18

course, this would not be the reason given when charges are filed . . .

We pulled into a filling station and stopped at the pump. It was a big station to be so far from town or village. A tall, sandy-haired white man came out smiling. He must have been about thirty. "What can I do for you?" he asked.

"May we use your rest rooms?"

"Sure thing! Right inside."

The men's room was immaculate. I called Clemmie. Surely there must have been a "colored" rest room around back. But the attendant didn't send us there. And we didn't look for it. When we came out, the tall white man was cleaning our windshield.

"Fill it up," I said, "and check the oil."

My wife and her sister slid out of the car.

The attendant stuck the nozzle of the hose into the tank and started cleaning the windows. Without missing a stroke, he asked, "What are you, a doctor?"

I pointed to the inverted clergy sign on the sun visor and said, "No. Minister."

"I thought you were something like that!"

A sixtyish-looking Negro, sitting on an empty soda crate, his fingers laced around his upraised knee, spat, shifted his cud, and said, "Yup. You can tell it every time. Had to be a professional man, all right."

The attendant asked, "Do you ever hear Billy Graham? Man, I could listen to that Billy all night. What kind of preacher are you?"

"Lutheran."

"What is that like?"

"Well, the order of service is similar to that of some Episcopal churches."

19

"O yes, we got one of those right over the road a piece. But mostly, ours are Methodist and Baptist. What do you think of this part of the country?"

I looked again at the green acres on rolling hills and said, "It looks like God's country to me! It reminds me of an old hymn."

He was such a pleasant fellow that even if he had asked me, I would not have told him that the hymn was "From Greenland's Icy Mountains," and the lines that came to mind a thousand times during our trip through the South were: ". . . where every prospect pleases, And only man is vile."

We bought cold drinks, cookies, potato chips, candy. We were in no hurry. It was a congenial place. Quite refreshed, we piled into the car. When I switched on the motor, the tall white man said, "You know, I think people are learning to get along better down here too."

We got lost in Montgomery, although we didn't know it. We were standing at a red light. Next to us was a new Ford station wagon. Sitting behind the wheel was a white man, about forty, wearing sun glasses. He yelled, "Going to Mobile?"

"Yes!" we chorused.

"Right highway. Wrong direction."

"What do we do, turn around?"

"Better follow me."

When the light changed we fell in behind the new station wagon. The traffic was heavy and following would have been difficult enough without all the turns we had to make.

Ruby said, "Pretty friendly, isn't he? I wonder if he belongs down here."

"He has an Alabama tag," I answered. "Still, he could

20

have come down with some of the new industries."

After about fifteen minutes through side streets and heavy traffic, we pulled once more into a main artery, and the Ford drew up at the entrance to a filling station. The driver got out, snatched off his glasses, and mopping his brow, walked over to the car.

"You see," he said, "many people get confused here. You were headed for Birmingham. Perhaps the confusion is caused by all the construction. A lot of that going on. The way you are now, you can keep straight ahead. A few miles out you will come to a fork. Construction work going on. Be sure to turn left. If you turn right you are going to head back toward Birmingham. Keep left and you will be OK. Have a good trip! I have to go back now, I'm a little late."

We thanked him as he walked away, and when he got into his station wagon, he waved and yelled, "Good luck!"

We waved back and pulled off in silence. There was no mistake about it. This man, who had evidently gone so far out of his way to do us a favor, spoke with an accent a man can acquire only when he is born and reared in Alabama.

A traffic officer in Mobile said that we could save several miles by using the new Bankhead Tunnel. It is a beautiful thing, a marvelous piece of engineering. As we drove through, I thought of Tallulah. Isn't it remarkable that a girl from Alabama can grow up to be so completely devoid of racial prejudice? She may have a great many weaknesses, but this does not seem to be one of them. Perhaps her book explains it. I will have to read it . . . someday.

In Mississippi we drove along the coast. On one side there were spacious homes and large guest houses, sitting behind a wall of ancient trees, trees of grotesque formations, trees

21

whose beards of moss almost dragged the ground. On the other side there were restaurants, frozen custard stands, and bath houses; and beyond, the white sand. Then, the broad, cool waters of the Sound.

They call it the Gold Coast, but to us it was the Great White Way. And I do mean white! Among the thousands of people we passed we saw only a handful of Negroes—a few women rolling their white folk's babies, and a few black-faced, white-coated boys working around the restaurants. We were told that we could find Negroes somewhere on the other side of the track, and Negro restaurants where we could buy food. But thanks to our front-seat carrier, we were not hungry, at least, not that hungry. In Mississippi we wanted to keep going.

I don't know why we were afraid. True, Reverend George T. Lee, who had refused to take his name off the Belzoni voters' list, had been shot to death. But we were not trying to get our names on a Mississippi voters' list. True, a Mississippi editor had said that the threat of violence is present whenever a Negro enters the courthouse to register. But we did not want to register, and we had no intention whatever of going near a courthouse. True, the White Citizens' Councils were intimidating Negroes and five gubernatorial candidates were campaigning on a Damn-the-Supreme-Court platform. But we did not intend to be there long enough to become involved.

When we analyzed the facts, we felt that our fears were groundless, for had not Mississippi shown that she was capable of compromise, Look at the evidence: for years one of the big sea food canneries had put out a product they called "Nigger Head Brand" oysters. After repeated pressure from the NAACP, the company made a noble concession. They changed the label to read, "Negro Head Brand" oysters.

22

Yes, perhaps our fears were groundless!

But this was before two white men beat in the face of a fourteen-year-old Negro boy with the butt of an Army automatic; before a mad white man shot a Negro child for allegedly insulting his half-brother's wife; before a group of Mississippi Christians, who praise God and profess faith in Jesus Christ, refused to indict two kidnapers who had already admitted the kidnaping! This was before *Look* magazine published an article naming the killers, but justifying their act in the eyes of prejudiced white men everywhere by making the dead Negro child guilty of the unpardonable crime of trying to hug a white man's wife! This was before the Till case . . . otherwise we would never have made this trip.

A spotlighted sign said: TOURIST INFORMATION, Map of City. I eased down on the brakes and nosed the car along the inclined shoulder of the highway. There was a long, low building, well lighted—a restaurant or beer parlor. As I approached I saw a sign across the lower part of the screen door. The large, crude letters said: COLORED SERVED IN REAR. I stopped in my tracks and began to look around. To the left and somewhat farther back there was the silhouette of a one-room building. Walking closer I noticed a signboard across the gable. I was unable to read it in the darkness, but it was long enough to carry the word INFORMATION, and probably did. The information office was closed for the night.

I turned back and walked toward the car, the clam shells crunching under my feet.

"Can I help you," someone shouted. It was a fat white woman standing in the door. The offensive sign now looked as though it were pinned to her skirt.

23

"I was looking for the information office," I said, and turned to go.

She answered, "Come on in. Charley had to go home, and he left his stuff with us."

I walked in when she threw the screen door open, followed her to a small counter at one end of the room, and told her what I wanted. She opened up a large city map and reached for her glasses.

The big room was long and narrow. Almost the entire length of one side was a counter that looked like a makeshift bar. The well-kept floor looked as though it might have been used occasionally for dancing, but now it held only a few scattered tables at which shirt-sleeved men sat smoking and drinking beer. The only woman in the place was the one who was poring over the map.

"Here it is," she said, and reached for a folder. She opened it up at a small map and carefully traced my route with a pencil. She was cheerful, smiling, courteous, and the entire service was rendered without a single trace of condescension. The shirt-sleeved men did not even notice my presence . . .

When I returned to the car I noticed an unusual commotion. Without opening the door, I stuck my head through the window and someone squirted sand into my face, or that is what I thought. I soon discovered that we had been attacked. My passengers were fighting for their lives. Wads of paper were flying everywhere, and still the mosquitoes poured in. When I opened the door to slip behind the wheel, the dome light went on. This betrayed our position to the squadrons soaring nearby, and they moved in mercilessly. I turned on the motor and, while backing out, threw open the vents as wide as they would go. In nothing flat, the needle on the speedometer climbed to sixty, and after a few minutes, the mosquitoes were gone. But we knew that they had been there, for our legs and arms and necks and faces were still burning.

Soon we were driving through a corridor of light as spectacular as a one-story Broadway, a seemingly endless string of roadhouses and motels, motels and roadhouses, on both sides of the highway. After awhile there appeared a short, black stretch in the middle of which a lonely neon sign flashed in fancy script: COLORED MOTEL. "Look," said my wife, "accommodations for Negro tourists—a colored motel!"

But I was not interested in a colored motel. This was the place of my birth. I was born and reared in New Orleans and still had many friends and relatives there. The pencil marks on my map would take me to the home of my oldest sister. I had a number . . . and a street name that I could not pronounce. On paper it looked like the slurring together of two cuss words that my memory dug up from the days of my labor with several New Orleans construction crews.

With all of the changes that had taken place in this city, I would have had a difficult time finding my sister's old home, the one uptown. But, she had written, that one was no longer there. The government had bought the site for a housing project and her husband had built a new home downtown, back o'town.

As I remembered it, this area was swampland. This was where we went to catch crawfish and mud turtles. This was where we caught snakes to sell to Joey, the young biologist who lived across the canal opposite our old home place. But the land had been drained and the city had bulged out to the very shores of Lake Pontchartrain. . . . I needed the pencil marks on the little city map.

A For Sale ad for my sister's new home would probably read: "Three large bedrooms, 1½ tiled baths, tiled kitchen, brick, originally built by contractor for own use."

It is an attractive home, and with all of the children gone, (the only unmarried one being with the Air Force in Germany), it offers more living space than my sister and her husband actually need.

Still, sitting between two small shotgun houses, backed to the cyclone fence by palmettoes and banana trees that stood above a tangled, semi-tropical undergrowth, it looked strangely out of place. It just didn't fit into its surroundings. Among the neat cottages that sat back on green lawns one block away, it would have been in perfect harmony with its setting. But that block was white . . .

When my wife noticed the method used to segregate Negroes in the New Orleans streetcars, she was at first offended, and then amused.

On each side of the aisle there is a piece of wood about two feet long, four inches wide, and one inch thick. On the bottom of this stick of wood—(for some reason they call it a screen)—there are two pegs which fit into corresponding holes found on the back of every seat in the car. On the back of this movable screen, stenciled in black letters, are the words: FOR COLORED PATRONS ONLY.

When a white person enters the car, he may move a screen toward the rear over as many empty seats as there are, as long as, when he attaches it, he sits in front of it. When a Negro comes in, he may move a screen toward the front over as many empty seats as there are, as long as, when he attaches it, he sits behind it, with the words, "For Colored Patrons Only" staring him in the face.

Janice, the youngest daughter of my deceased brother, explained it like this: "You see, Aunt Glenice, here in New Orleans there are so many white black people, and so many black white people, that no one knows who is what. With these screens, each streetcar rider can classify himself!"

Of course, every now and then a screen disappears—thrown out by an angry rider, or stolen as a souvenir by an out-of-town visitor. At times, too, they have come in handy for streetcar fights. In fact, the oldtimers say that when the section known as the Irish Channel was in bloom, streetcar screens were hoarded as shillelaghs. Buddie, my sister's husband, said that a giant Negro—(a stereotyped expression used by Southern papers in reporting Negro crimes)—a giant Negro got on a streetcar in the Irish Channel one night and began singing. Several men cocked their ears, listened for awhile, then snatched up the screens and beat the big black man to death. He had been singing, "Ireland Must be Heaven 'Cause My Mother Came from There."

Since Buddie is not known for his veracity, I hardly knew how to take this tale of the olden days in the Irish Channel. When a sheepish grin stretched across his face, I began to doubt. When he squinted one eye and raised the brow of the other, I didn't believe him. When he laughed out loud and said, "And that's the truth!" I knew he was lying.

The day we had set aside for a visit to the old French Quarter began as a washout. We had just finished breakfast when the heavens were opened and the rain came down in torrents. As we left the table, my wife said, as if speaking to herself, "No Vieux Carré today."

"Why not?" answered my sister. "Look," she said, and walking across the living room she pulled the door open. On the other side of the street the sun was shining.

"Here in New Orleans," my sister explained, "when you want to go, you go. We don't let summer showers stop us.

In the French Quarter it may be as dry as a bone."

After awhile the torrents ceased, the sky became overcast, and a steady drizzle settled over the city. This we could take.

We had planned to walk through the Vieux Carré, but because of the weather we decided to risk using the car. And luck was with us. Since I was there last, parking meters had been installed along Royal Street, and behind Saint Louis Cathedral, at the entrance to Pirate's Alley, we found a place to park. We fed a nickel to the parking meter and ran through the alley to the cathedral.

In spite of the drizzle there were scores of tourists in the ancient church. We joined one of the groups, and following our guide, listened in silence as he chanted the colorful history of this old edifice erected on a site which Bienville himself had marked off with his sword.

We went next to the Cabildo, erected in 1795 as a meeting place for the Spanish rulers. Here, in this old building next to the famous Catholic cathedral, began the first Protestant services ever held in Louisiana. Here the Louisiana Purchase was consummated. Today, however, the Cabildo is a state museum.

Somehow we lost Clemmie in the Cabildo. When we found him, he was standing wide-eyed before an exhibit of old-fashioned guns.

When we reached the death mask of Napoleon Bonaparte, I darted out and ran through Pirate's Alley to put another nickel into the parking meter. The sun was out, and the artists of Pirate's Alley were stretching their pictures along the cathedral fence.

It was Clemmie who insisted on walking through Jackson's Square. I don't know what fascinated him more—Jackson on horseback, or the horse. When he was satisfied, we left the square, walked past the Pontalba Building, and through Saint Anthony's Alley.

On the downtown side of the street three Negro nuns appeared. In the middle of the block they turned into a door and vanished. I had almost forgotten this old building, but slowly it came back to me. It was here that I had visited Sister Virginia.

We had stopped to survey the place from the opposite side of the street. "That building," I said, "dates back almost to the days of Napoleon."

A lean figure walked hurriedly down the banquette to the convent door. As if by some prearranged signal, the door opened and a brown-skinned arm reached out with a half-wrapped po' boy sandwich. The lean man took the sandwich, made a neat about-face, and walked hurriedly away.

"That building," I went on, "used to be . . ."

"Hey, mister!" a finger tapped my shoulder, "got two bits for a bite to eat?"

When I turned, I looked into a pair of blood-shot eyes staring out of a bony face over a beard of several days' growth.

"See that convent over there," I said. "If you go over and ask, the sisters will give you something to eat."

"Bad stomach," he answered, "can't eat the stuff they have. . . . Tourists, huh? Know the story of that building? It's worth two bits, yes. The Marquis de Lafayette was entertained there. The State Legislature met there for a while. And then," his voice became a stage whisper—"there were the famous quadroon balls. Every year at a certain time the pretty quadroon girls were dressed in their finest and escorted to the ball by their mothers. The rich, young dandies were accompanied by their fathers. Then the boy

29

selected himself a pretty quadroon and set her up in an apartment on Rampart Street. The fathers arranged it this way to tide their sons over until the time of marriage."

"And what happened to the Negro girls when the young men married?" Ruby asked.

"And now," the man rattled on as if he hadn't heard, "the building is a convent, occupied by a group of colored nuns who, by daily prayers and good works, seek to expiate the sins of their forbears."

His recitation ended, his shaking hand reached for the quarter. The story was worth it. He turned and walked away like a man leaning against the wind. He was in a hurry . . . a big hurry! . . . No wonder he couldn't eat the stuff the sisters had. They didn't hand out sherry sandwiches . . .

I wished that he had answered Ruby's question. And then, too, I had one to ask him: Who is expiating the sins of those young dandies and their fathers . . . ?

Before the day was over we looked into Old Absinthe House and walked past Antoine's, but we didn't stop for dinner. In fact, when we went to the French market to buy a turtle—(Ruby had never tasted *cowan*)—we didn't eat there either, although we parked only a few yards from their open-air restaurant. . . . We saw no accommodations for Negroes . . .

The morning we drove up to the old home place I was quite unprepared for the things I saw and the ugly mood that followed.

We drove uptown on Claiborne Avenue and turned back at Erato. I lifted my foot off the gas and rolled along in amazement. Suddenly I stopped. I was completely lost. We were standing in the middle of a broad, paved street. For blocks around there were large, brick apartment buildings placed symmetrically around lawns, walks and play areas. It looked like something right off the planning board. It looked like a park . . . and a passerby said that it was—Miro Parkway. The buildings were government project houses.

No wonder I couldn't find the landmarks. Lang's junk-yard was gone. The soupy streets, where mud squeezed through the toes of shoeless boys, were paved. Curtis's house, where Stovepipe Joe sat on a flagpole for peanuts and popularity, had vanished.

And the city dump—what had become of that? Where were the acres of shining tin cans, saying: This is Silver City? Where was the refuse, the dirt, the filth, the stench? What became of the women who picked rags for a living—the men who searched the garbage for slop for their pigs and the boys who picked bottles and bones to sell to Lang for Jumbo money and movie fare? Surely, all of this could not have happened since the last time I was here! . . . Come to think of it, yes, it could. The last time I was here I didn't see this section. I was here on business, and my business was elsewhere . . .

We turned uptown again and drove along Galvez Street to Melpomene. And there it happened.

I was in the middle of the rickety, wooden bridge that crossed the drainage canal. The Negro driver tumbled from his dump cart, and a red-faced white man jumped from his horse. The white dumpmaster was holding a gun in his left hand and swinging a mule whip with his right. He lashed the cart-driver for all he was worth—back, arms, legs. The Negro staggered up, and with the palms of his hands facing out, because of the gun, tried to ward off the lash with his elbows. But still it came over his arms, legs, back, neck and face. The Negro began backing up, back over the gutter, over the banquette, up the steps (the blows still falling), back across the gallery of the little gray house. The screen door flew open, the Negro backed in, and a small, black woman stepped out, slammed the door and leaned against it, feet planted and arms akimbo. The dumpmaster kept his gun leveled, but letting his mule whip drag, backed down the steps and across the banquette and gutter. Leaping to his saddle, he turned and rode full gallop past an enraged teen-ager standing on the bridge.

It was a long, long time ago when this happened. The rickety old bridge is no longer there. The canal still runs, but through a concrete tunnel. Only the little, old house is there. Why the sight of this weather-beaten shack should conjure up this picture to kick me in the stomach, I don't know. Was it, perhaps, because of the effect it had on me when it happened? Was it because on that day in my early teens, for the first time in my life, I felt the urge to kill?

The ugly mood I was in dragged back other incidents that made me angry enough to kill.

When I was in the seminary I spent several summers working in a resort at the seashore. I was night man at a hotel. I came in at midnight and, working alone, had to operate the elevator, take care of room guests who checked in late, and provide services requested by insomniacs.

One night I got a call for a pitcher of ice. When I had blocked the door of my elevator and walked into the room, I found eight or ten men there. They had been drinking heavily.

"Come on, boy. Have a drink!" one of them slobbered.

"No, thanks," I said and moved toward the ice bucket on the table.

Someone else joined in, "Come on, have a drink!"

"No, thanks," I repeated, "I have work to do."

32

"Come on, boy. It's good stuff!" Others were attracted.

"What's the matter? He thinks he's too good to drink with us." It was getting to be a game.

"No, I have work to do," I said, and emptying my pitcher, I turned to leave the room.

Two men were barring the door. Suddenly someone spun me around by the shoulder, and my arms were pinned to my sides. Others crowded in and held me there . . . and the slobbering bald-head who had started it all, poured a water glass of whiskey down my throat.

What could I do? I have a friend who was shot in an identical situation.

And another experience came to mind. It was in the same hotel, but during a different season.

Long after midnight a young woman came in. She must have been about thirty. She was well-dressed and attractive. A *Daily News* reporter would call her beautiful. She walked into the elevator and said, "Four, please." I stopped at four and opened the door. When she stepped into the hall, she turned quickly and said, "Will you bring me some ice?"

About twenty minutes later, after several interruptions, I knocked on her door. When she opened it, she stood there dressed in a pair of pink bedroom slippers . . . and that was all.

The hair on her head was blonde. She said, "You'll find my pitcher in the bath," and walked ahead.

When I came out of the bathroom she was standing before a full-length mirror, nonchalantly brushing her shoulder bob.

In the South I had heard tales of rich, white women calling the Negro butler into the bathroom and asking him to scrub her back! Frankly, I didn't believe it. But now it was happening to me. What did this woman take me for? A

33

woman might act like this before a house pet walking around in the room, but not before a strange man. That's the point! To her I was a dog!

Without missing a stroke of the brush, she said, "You'll find a quarter on the dresser." She sang it . . . sang it in soft Southern accents.

That was a quarter I didn't need. This hussy had emasculated me! When I slammed the door my stomach bounced my food into my throat . . .

Bernadine, a younger sister, was sitting on the gallery when we arrived at the old home place. Soon we had all settled there to catch what we could of the morning breeze.

This wasn't much like going home. With the exception of the old house itself, and the one next door, which I myself had built before leaving for the seminary, there was nothing of the past.

Across the canal I should have seen the Leonards' home, the big white house almost surrounded by banana trees, tall corn, and a high board fence. The Leonards were our nearest white neighbors, and Joey, their only son, was the brilliant young biologist who bought the snakes that we caught in the swamps. I was sitting on this very gallery the day they took Joey away. He hesitated under the grapevine that hung over the high front steps, then walked through the gate of the iron picket fence to a model-T Ford that stood in the street. This was a black day in the big white house across the canal. But what else could they do? The young biologist had begun taking sneak shots at his mother with a .22 rifle. . . . Joey's white mother was heartbroken, and many black women suffered with her, for these neighbors were mothers too.

The gate opened and a young man walked in, tall, brown-skinned. He was an attorney, engaged to marry my niece.

34

When we were introduced he shook hands and said, "Well, what do you think of your old neighborhood?"

I looked at the concrete top on the old drainage canal and the big apartment buildings stretching as far as the eye could see, and replied, "Where is it? . . . You know," I continued, "I have been wondering how this city can still get funds for segregated housing. I feel that public funds for segregated housing ought to be discontinued."

"Perhaps so," he answered, "but is there any anti-segregation ruling that the South will not try to circumvent? Here in New Orleans we are not building new projects, but extending the old ones."

"Speaking of circumvention," my sister joined in, "what about the segregation laws passed by the South itself? When it is to a white man's advantage, he either circumvents them or deliberately ignores them. Look how they chase after Negro women . . ."

We were in the living room when my niece came in. She took me by surprise, and I had to make small talk about her wedding plans to keep my eyes from betraying me. She is the spitting image of her father, and in her, I saw him.

My brother and I had attended the same parochial school. We were confirmed at the same altar. I became a carpenter. He became a plasterer. I went away to the seminary. He stayed home and married.

Things went well for a while, and then the depression struck. Work became scarce. White men who had never worked with their hands began to take over any job they could get. As Negroes were pushed farther and farther down the ladder, my brother found a job on the waterfront. This too was irregular, and as things grew worse he began to drink.

One night he came home in a drunken rage. Through torrents of tears he shouted, "If there is a God in heaven, He must be a white man, or why would He let me and my family suffer like this."

His wife quieted him down, and with great effort got him to bed. After hours of fitful sleep, he began to mumble, "O, Almighty God, merciful Father, I, a poor, miserable sinner, confess unto Thee all my sins and . . ."

One day he shook himself to death in my mother's arms.

The day we drove through the campus of Dillard University roofers were winding up their work on the new chapel. I remembered this area, for less than a mile away I had helped to build a home for the wife of a white bootlegger who was doing time, because, as he put it, he had not paid off the right people. This area was wooded then, and marked off from the suburbs by a dusty clamshell road.

We went next to Xavier University, a Catholic school for Negro youth. The buildings were locked and the grounds deserted. Clemmie, who had already informed us that he had seen enough schools to last him the rest of his life, was delighted. He said, "Good. Now, let's get going. You promised to take us to the aquarium." Junior, one of Buddie's grand-children, a year younger than Clemmie, was equally anxious to keep moving. We had promised to take them to Audubon Park. These side excursions, while on our route, were an unnecessary waste of time. Nevertheless, there was something else we wanted to see en route to the park—the home of Huey P. Long.

When Northern papers were denouncing Long as a demagogue and Southern papers were crying foul play, there were thousands of little people, honest men and women, black and white, who were willing to follow wherever he led. If historians discount everything else that Long did, they will still have to give him credit for making the man on the street conscious of the affairs of government. In New Orleans there are still people who speak of him with an admiration that borders on reverence, and repeat tales of the good that he did.

Buddie tells of the time a committee of local Negroes waited on the Kingfish in his downtown office. They told him that there were many Negro girls who were registered nurses and many more still in training. These Negro girls, however, were not able to get employment as nurses at the Charity Hospital. They wondered whether the governor could do something about it.

"Well, gentlemen," he replied, "I don't know what I will be able to do. When colored girls are prepared for nursing, they ought to be given a decent opportunity to practice their profession. Tell you what! I'll see what I can do. But you know these white people around here as well as I do—only I have ways of handling them. I'm with you, gentlemen, but remember, I have to use my own methods. After all, what you want is action."

A few days later, Buddie said, the Kingfish made a surprise inspection tour of the hospital, giving special attention to Negro wards. The inspection over, he stormed into the office, boiling. "This is a hell of a come-off!" he shouted. "What's the idea of having our white ladies handling all these nigger men? Aren't there any nigger nurses? This thing's got to stop!"

As I said before, you don't always know how to take Buddie. I waited for the squinted eye and raised brow, but it didn't show. I thought once that I saw a flicker of that fish-tale grin, but it was only a flicker. So, to this day, I am not certain. I don't know exactly how it came about. But this much is true: Negro nurses are working at the Charity Hospital . . .

Huey P. Long's old home is a showplace and local people like to talk about it. But when we reached the site I had lost the capacity to appreciate it, for I suddenly remembered that this was the area in which one of my sisters had been injured when she jumped from an automobile into which she had been dragged by a drunken white man . . .

The park was crowded that day. We left the car under the shade of a tree and walked in the broiling sun from cage to cage and from pen to pen until our clothes were soaked and our feet were aching.

I was saving the aquarium until last. That was to be the climax. I had seen it when I was a child and had told Clemmie and Junior that we would see strange denizens of the deep; big fish that swoop right out at you, only to be stopped by their plate-glass enclosures, and alligators swimming in a big pool right in the middle of the floor.

Somehow the aquarium was hard to find. I was certain now that it had been demolished, for there was nothing in sight as large as the building I remembered. I couldn't believe it when a guard insisted that this was it—this tiny, tile-topped thing we had walked past twice.

Some of the little tanks were empty, and those in use held fish that were small and colorless. The big pool in the middle of the floor was now a little puddle, and there wasn't even a tadpole in it. My disappointment was relieved only by the laughter in Clemmie's eyes, when he said, "Mamma, Daddy goofed again, didn't he!"

Clemmie began asking for something to drink the moment we passed the first lunch stand. The truth of the matter is that under the hot Louisiana sun we were all thirsty, but I insisted that, since there was a lot more to see, we'd better keep moving; perhaps we would stop and get something later.

Really, I didn't know what to do. I was looking for a lunch stand at which a Negro was being served, then I would know that it was safe. But so far the only Negroes we had seen in the park were two workmen scrubbing a pool.

I had heard of the girl who, finding herself in the shopping district with a splitting headache, stopped at a drugstore to get some BC tablets and a coke. They gave her the BCs, and while they were drawing the coke she threw two tablets into her mouth. She took the paper cup and raised it to her lips, but before she could drink it the jerk behind the counter yelled, "You can't drink that in here! Take it outside!"

One has to be careful. A Negro never knows his "place." Of course, there are some general rules, but these general rules vary from town to town and from white man to white man. In the final analysis, the Negro's place is wherever any white man, in whatever mood, under whatever condition, in a split second, may decide. And the Negro is supposed to respond accordingly!

Take my Louisiana friend, for instance, the one with that enviable head of wavy brown hair. One day he went into an office building and found himself standing before a desk at which a young white woman was working. Of course, he had removed his hat. That was in keeping with the general rule. When the young white woman looked up to ask my friend what he wanted, she began to stare at his hair. Someone shouted from across the room, "Hey you! Put your hat on!" It was a bald-headed white man.

One has to be careful. But we had now come to the aquarium, and there was only one more lunch stand between us and the car. There was no sign saying WHITE ONLY.

39

Neither was there a sign saying COLORED SERVED IN REAR. There was no Negro standing before the counter to indicate the "place" and remove the fear.

I whispered to my wife, "You take the others back to the car, and I will see if I can get some sandwiches and something to drink."

As a starter, I ordered a container of ice cream. That came up in a paper bag, as if the man didn't intend for me to eat it there. Taking this as my cue, I ordered sandwiches and drinks "to go."

We sat at the car in the shade of a tree, eating our lunch and watching the laughing youngsters swimming in a pool about a hundred fifty yards away. No embarrassing questions were raised about that. Clemmie no longer likes the water . . . and Junior had better sense than to ask. . . .

We took the ferry at Marrero and crossed the Mississippi. Although old landmarks were scarce, I showed Clemmie where my father and I used to row across the river at night on cat-fishing trips, and pointed out the racing whirlpools that, like conflicting currents of life, used to strike our little skiff and send us where we had not planned to go.

From Marrero we drove to Algiers and crossed the river again. The Algiers ferry gave us another view of the waterfront and the odd, low skyline of what is said to be the nation's most interesting city. But the only thing we could identify was Saint Louis Cathedral. We could see the spires in the distance.

We drove off the ferry where Canal Street begins and back up Canal until we came to some of the most beautiful cemeteries we had ever seen. When Ruby saw the miniature marble castles in this city of the dead, she said, "Now I remember it. This is the city in which the dead are buried above the earth. I remember reading that somewhere. The reason given was that the ground is too wet . . ."

"Yes," I interrupted, "But that is only partly true. Not all the dead are buried above the ground. I don't know how they handle the problem of seeping water today, but I have seen gravediggers hold a floating coffin down with poles until they could throw in enough mud to keep it down. Of course, that kind of grave doesn't look good on a postcard."

Near one of these cemeteries I expected to find the basin, the old boat canal that led to Lake Pontchartrain. I couldn't imagine what had happened. Surely it was too big a thing for me to miss. It was here that we went fishing when we couldn't go all the way to Bucktown. It was through this canal that barges and schooners brought their goods into the heart of the city. Through this canal we used to enter the lake in the sleek cabin-cruiser that my marine-mechanic cousin kept in condition while its white owner was doing nine months for rum-running. . . . It was too big a thing to vanish. But it had! When we reached West End, where the canal enters the lake, we discovered the reason why. There was an army of men at work filling in the last half mile . . .

At West End I knew that I had goofed again, long before Clemmie said anything about it. I intended to show him the ridgetop footpath that we used to follow on our way to the boathouse at Bucktown. But how could he see the narrow footpath on this broad, tree-lined avenue? How could he hear the swamp's nighttime symphony, undergirded by the booming bass of the bullfrogs, in the midst of these honking auto horns? Clemmie couldn't even understand that my father always carried the lantern, because when I carried it, it attracted mosquitoes to my long, skinny legs. In fact, he pressed the point—Didn't I wear pants? And if so, why weren't the legs of my pants as long as my dad's, since the mosquitoes didn't sting his legs, did they?

41

The swamp was gone. From West End to Bucktown there were broad, paved streets . . . and palm trees waving in the breeze that came in from the lake. Near Bucktown, restaurants and dancehalls and amusement stands lined the shore. But this was white—all white. Under a blaring loudspeaker, pouring out a canned jazz that would have made Louis Armstrong deny the city of his birth, a teen-age white boy told us that colored people had their own place, way, way down the lakefront. They called it Lincoln Beach . . . he thought.

I saw Lincoln Beach, but it was quite by accident. A young insurance executive drove me out to see Pontchartrain Park, a new residential development for Negroes. I soon discovered that Pontchartrain Park was chiefly on paper. But there was sufficient evidence of the fact that a start had been made. There were a number of ranch-style houses—perhaps ten or twelve—sitting back on newly-sown lawns. Some were model houses open for inspection. Others, the young man said, had been sold.

Before one of the models there was a sand-table miniature of the proposed project. In the center, shaped like a gigantic teardrop, was a park bordered by a broad, paved road. Along this road around the park, home sites were laid out. According to the plans, when this community is completed it will have an 18-hole golf course, a clubhouse and stadium, a swimming pool, and picnic grounds. On paper it may well be, as one of the promotion folders boasted, one of the best-planned neighborhoods in the nation.

"What do you think of it?" the insurance man asked.

"Wonderful," I replied.

Interrupting, he continued, "You see, when a man buys a home, he also buys atmosphere. These homes will cost from ten to twenty-five thousand dollars. But it will be a community of homes in this price range. The Negro's choice of a home site is definitely limited, no matter what the courts say about restrictive covenants. So a man often finds himself building his dream house next to a shack. . . . But you know how that is . . ."

Yes, I knew. I knew also that it was practically the same all over the country. I thought of Harlem, often referred to as the white man's sin, and of all the little Harlems in the big cities of the North. And hadn't we spent almost a year trying to find living quarters for a pastor who, for a time, was my assistant? There were many houses and apartments available, but whenever we appeared on the scene, they had just been rented. I remembered the time I got a rental agent on the phone. Yes, they had a vacant apartment—"But, frankly, Pastor, if you want it for your assistant, I don't think it would be suitable. You see, the building is full of dirty Irish." But we were desperate for shelter. I told him that we were up against it and I would like to see the place anyway.

There was a long silence, and then the agent asked, "Tell me, Pastor, is your assistant white or colored?"

When I said "colored," the agent blurted, "Well they wouldn't want him there!"

In spite of all that, Negroes have bought homes and rented apartments in white neighborhoods. In many cases they were deliberately planted. And once they moved in the cry went up, "The Negroes are coming!" The flames of racial prejudice were often fanned by the owners or agents themselves, because they knew that they could get several times more money from Negroes than they were getting from the whites. So blocks were "busted," white people fled the "black plague," and Harlems were born.

Look at what is happening in Westchester. And look at

43

Long Island today. The more Negroes move into Long Island, the farther out the white people move. What is going to happen when they are crowded to the water's edge? Will we see a new species of lake dwellers?

I am sure that there are white people who sell or rent homes to Negroes in white neighborhoods with the purest of motives. But too often it is like that case in New Jersey:

A white man built a new home on the outer edge of the suburbs. This was just the thing. Now he could get what he had always wanted—a riding horse. But shortly after he built the stable and bought a horse the neighbors began complaining. Hot words began to fly and the neighbors became downright disagreeable and almost impossible to live with. The man became vindictive. If he couldn't live there and like it, they couldn't either. . . . He sold the place to a Negro . . .

"I wonder," I said to the young executive, "about the Negro market for homes like these. I have found a great deal of uncertainty, and so many Negroes are leaving the South . . ."

"That may be true," he responded, "but that has been going on for a good many years. Remember the first World War—And then look at the great exodus during World War II. To a greater or lesser degree, it is a containing process. When one looks at the conditions under which Negroes live in the large cities of the North, and even out West, he has to wonder why they do it. You know the answer. They are searching for a place where they can breathe free. Whether or not they find it is another matter."

"I know of the black ghettos of the North," I replied, "I know of the economic and social restrictions, too."

"Yes," he went on, "but at least there *the law is not stacked against you*. But . . . but look at the South today. With its mild climate, wide-open spaces and growing in-

44

dustries—what more could a man want? Most of the Negroes don't want to leave the South. That is the land of their birth . . . and it might well be the future of the country . . .

"There are some Negroes who are not going to leave the South, no matter what happens. They have learned, at times by trial and error, that in a certain community they may go to this church and that school, this store and that market, get this job, and enter that theater. Having learned their 'place,' they have accepted it. Here they feel comparatively safe. So they walk this route until it becomes their rut, and no matter what happens, they are going to stay right there and wear their rut deep enough to make it their grave.

"And this is what the white man wants—Negroes in their place. The Southern white man doesn't want to deal with Negroes on human terms. If he did, then there would be nobody for him to feel superior to.

"Still . . . there are many Negroes in the South who want to stay in the South because, in spite of their heartache, they have cherished a hope—the hope of one day achieving acceptance as human beings.

"Not long ago a light burst into the darkness and we thought it meant the coming of the day. When the Supreme Court handed down its desegregation decision, we were as happy as children on a merry-go-round. We thought the path was laid out when so many high church officials reviewed the decision favorably. But look what happened. The rebels yelled and frightened the frocks off the clergymen. Reaction set in. Hate-mongers at first felt their way, and then, finding no resistance, let go with all they had. Negroes are starved into submission. Homes are burned or bombed. Oh, I know that there are good white people in the South. But some of them are now beginning to feel the fear that Negroes have lived with all their lives. They are scared to open their mouths. Regardless, to many Negroes, the South is home! Here they want to work and buy and build. Here they live . . . and here they want to die . . ."

When we had driven out to Lake Pontchartrain Park, this young man was the picture of composure. He was pleasant, at times even gay . . . quite sure of himself. But now his eyes flashed fire and his face was as hard as granite. He threw away one cigarette and lit another.

"I know," I said, "that men are reluctant to pull up stakes and . . ."

"But it happens!" he snapped back. "There was a brilliant young doctor here a few years ago. He had a wife and two boys. His wife was his laboratory technician . . ."

"What was his name?" I asked.

There was an awkward pause, and then he said, "Johnson . . . Dr. Johnson . . . He bought a home, established a good practice, and was one of the finest citizens in the community. But one evening, after a hard day's work, his wife suggested that they go out for an airing, just the two of them. His wife was driving—to keep in practice she said. Out near the lakefront she became tired. So she pulled off the road and the doctor got out, walked around the car, and slid in under the wheel. His wife pulled out a cigarette, and he reached over to light it for her! Just then a light flashed in. There were two policemen behind it. First they tried bullying the doctor, fishing for a handout. But the doctor wouldn't bite. So the dirty bas— the policemen took them in and charged them with using a parked car for immoral purposes! The doctor was so disgusted that he sold out and left town."

I wanted to say that I knew this doctor. This refugee from behind the cotton curtain was a friend of mine. I knew exactly where he had settled in our Eastern Zone. I wanted to

46

say that; but why continue the discussion? The young man had lied. He had deliberately falsified my friend's name. Why? What was the reason? Was he afraid of something? Afraid, perhaps, that those two white policemen, foiled in an attempted shakedown, could somehow reach out and harm the doctor again? . . .

"Lincoln Beach is not far away," he said, "I would like to take you there."

Lincoln Beach—yes, that's the place the teen-age boy had mentioned. Perhaps I ought to see it.

This lakefront recreation park was new. In fact, one of the buildings was still under construction. It looked like a dancehall. There must have been several thousand people there that day. There were gay couples strolling on the sand, laughing youngsters splashing in the water, screeching children in toy autos, and people just sitting around, laughing and talking.

"Look," I said, "the carefree, happy-go-lucky Negro. Not a care in the world!"

"Come, let me show you something," the insurance man said.

We barged into a small circle of young men and women standing in front of a refreshment stand. The insurance man introduced himself and then said, "My friend here is from New York City. He wants to know what you think about the segregation-integration question."

The laughing stopped. Every smile vanished. There was a sickening silence . . . until one man said, "Do you think these white people down here want to integrate? See this beach? See these buildings here? Why do you think they gave them to us? To keep us away from theirs, that's why. That's why they started building new schools for colored. They don't want us. . . . We're dogs to them—dogs—you

47

hear me? These new buildings are crumbs from the master's table. With these the dogs are supposed to be satisfied."

We tried this on several other groups and the reaction was the same. There were a few who evidently resented this intrusion. They hated us for having tricked them into dropping their mask . . . interrupting their escape.

"You see," said the insurance man, "there is your gay, carefree Negro. Laughing, yes, but laughing just to keep from crying. And these same people you see here are the devout, deeply religious Negroes you hear white people talking about. They are religious all right—good Christians! But their Christianity is just like the white man's—it stinks to high heaven."

"Aren't you a Christian?" I asked.

He wasn't ready for this. I took him by surprise, and he didn't like it.

"Well . . . yes," he said . . . "at least, I was . . . Catholic. . . . I became a Catholic. But it didn't do any good. It didn't bring me any closer to Catholics—not white ones, anyway. I know the teachings of the Church. I know the fine statements made by high Catholic officials; Protestants, too. But the man in the pulpit isn't opening his mouth. Catholics and Protestants alike go right on discriminating, go right on sweating your blood out, go right on letting any white man, even if he is as sinful as Satan, spit on any colored man, even if he is as holy as Mary. When I became a Catholic I thought I would find peace. But if there is any peace of God that passes all understanding, I didn't find it. The little peace I found was kicked right out of me by my fellow Christians. I had become a Catholic, but I hadn't become a human being. I had become a Catholic, but I was only a black Catholic, just as you are a black Lutheran . . . and neither of us will ever be accepted as anything more . . ."

48

Before we turned to go, we took one last look at Lincoln Beach. . . . Then we left these black sons of the South . . . these dogs with their crumb . . .

The last time I saw the Union Station in New Orleans was the year I went down on vacation and spent the time building a house.

When I got off the Jim Crow car and walked toward the station I saw a lively crowd of people semi-circled around a tiny woman. Approaching from the rear, where the crowd was thinnest, I soon got close enough to see a living doll. It was Dolores Del Rio, arriving in town for the premier of *Evangeline.* Around her there were young girls staring in envy, men, frog-eyed and drooling, and sober-faced women, disgusted over watching the male of the species making an ass of himself.

As far as white women were concerned, I had trained myself to think blank. This was safe . . . this was my "place." The white men could stare and comment and undress her with their eyes, but in their presence, a black man had to see and yet not see, judge and yet have no opinion. For a black man to look at a white woman—queen or prostitute—and note her three essential measurements, was unthinkable. To imagine what she looked like with her clothes off was plain sacrilege. My "place" was to stand as though in The Presence . . . to look with holy reverence. . . . I walked away . . .

Even in those days there was occasional talk of a new Union Station. It was one of those things the city needed, but it was always an objective to be achieved on some indefinite tomorrow. So I was pleasantly surprised last summer when someone asked, "Have you seen our new station?"

In the heavy evening traffic we were waved ahead by a Negro traffic cop—another New Orleans improvement. We swung around a big statue of Bienville and angled up to the curb. Leaving the car, we walked through the colored entrance into the waiting room.

This was a modern palace. There was one broad room that stretched the width of the building. The immaculate floor, the neat rows of comfortable seats, the shining metal trimming, looked as though they had kept a spit-and-polish crew working overtime. If ever there were equal but opposite facilities, here they were! The only thing that separated the white half of this big room from the colored half was a small souvenir stand.

My mind was racing ahead to the toilets, the water fountains, the dining facilities. I wanted to see how the New South was handling these delicate matters. But suddenly I forgot all about these details. . . . I saw something that excited me.

On the walls near the ceiling there were four panels of murals depicting, in order, the Age of Exploration, the Age of Colonization, the Age of Conflict, and the Modern Age. It was the Modern Age that excited me. Among other things, it presented two men, one black and one white, and two women, one black and one white, sitting side by side in the same classroom. And—there was a white man standing next to a Negro man in what appeared to be "social equality!"

Was this another illustration of the fact that poets and artists seem to have a deeper insight into social trends than do educators and politicians? Was this another bit of evidence that these queer people often have a clearer picture of the eternal rightness of things than do our clergymen? Or was it that some impish muse had compelled the artist to paint he knew not what?

Yes, it was strange that in a State that threatened to use its police power to retain its system of segregation, a painting like this should be displayed. Strange that in a city where schools are separate and Negro citizens are forced to ride behind streetcar screens saying, "For Colored Patrons Only," strange that in such a city one would find this significant mural in a public waiting room.

I wondered who had approved it. Was it a city father poking fun at ignorant, lily-white voters? Was it some sympathetic official's way of holding out hope to suffering Negroes? Was it some cautious railroad executive who felt safe in the act because he knew that hate-mongers who can hardly read would never stop to study the meaning of a complex mural? Or was the approval given, perhaps, by a Committee of the Timid Righteous who used this method of confessing their sins and purging their consciences? . . . Most likely I shall never know. . . . Somewhat exhausted, I went back to the car without inspecting the rest of the station.

On Sunday my niece drove me to church, my home church, the oldest Negro Lutheran church in the city of New Orleans.

The pastor had called the evening before to offer me his pulpit. I had preached there several times before. But my mother was always there. Would I be able to look out from the pulpit and see the people present, or would I see my mother in her pew, the younger children beside her? Would I be able to retain my composure if, in the midst of my sermon, I suddenly saw the trouble that the hand of time had etched into the face of a childhood playmate? Could I concentrate on what I had to say, or would I be searching for faces no longer there—Old man Rousseau, Mrs. Luecke, the Elder Fisher, Mother Wright? I wasn't feeling well, anyway . . . and I was afraid that my heart might play tricks with my eyes. Who can listen to a crying preacher?

51

I declined the pastor's invitation to preach and agreed to assist him at communion. This would give me an opportunity to worship with the congregation.

The church building looked the same and was still in fairly good condition. But to me, the schoolhouse across the yard looked pitiful. Even when I was a child, it was inadequate. . . . It reminded me of the ancient chapel beside our Parish House in New York City. Both ought to be torn down and carted away. But new buildings cost money, a lot of money! . . . What can you do when people give from the top of their pockets, rather than from the bottom of their hearts?

The only white person in church that day was the young unmarried pastor. But that could hardly be considered an evidence of integration, because white pastors have served Negro congregations from the very beginning. Often white pastors have entered Negro work against the opposition of their friends and the tears of their mothers. Usually the opposition died away, the tears evaporated, and the friends and relatives began thinking of the white pastors in Negro congregations as foreign missionaries, sacrificing their lives for the propagation of the faith. However, I have still to meet a white pastor worthy of his salt who accepted this mantle of martyrdom conferred upon him by family and friends . . .

No, the presence of the white pastor did not mean integration. In fact, the organized Christian Church seems to be the body that is least concerned about integration. Resolutions are passed. Statements are prepared and published. But there is very little day-by-day effort to bring the various racial groups together around a common pulpit or before a common communion rail.

This in itself would be bad enough. But it indicates something deeper. Men and women and children who refuse to worship together are certainly not inclined to study together in the same schools, eat together in the same restaurants, live together in the same communities, and work together as equals on the same jobs. Thus, these people must of necessity strengthen the social and economic system that brings suffering and death to Negro Americans, disgrace to the name of Christ, and weakness to the country they profess to love . . .

A year or so ago I read a book called *Race and Religion*. The author argued that Jesus was not a Jew but an Aryan. Christianity, therefore, is an Aryan religion and only Aryans are naturally susceptible to the Christian faith. As proof of this, he pointed out that after two thousand years of missionary work, there are comparatively few non-Aryan converts. I don't know what brought it to mind, but I was thinking about this after service at my old home church.

Let me say that I don't agree with the author of *Race and Religion*. Yet there are white people who act as though Christianity is an Aryan religion, at least, *their* conception of Christianity. Their trouble is, I believe, that they have not accepted the whole Word of God. They act as though they got stuck at the sentence: "All things are yours." And that is the word by which they live.

And the Negroes—what about them? Do they accept the whole Word of God, or do they too get stuck at a certain passage? If so, what is it—"All things will work together for good," or "Vengeance is Mine; I will repay, saith the Lord?" . . . What would happen in the South, I wondered—in the whole country, for that matter—if the people who profess faith in Christ would really accept Christianity as a way of life? . . .

On the way home we passed the Municipal Auditorium.

The place was still standing! It was still being used! Nothing, absolutely nothing had happened to it!

Perhaps I had better explain the reason for my surprise.

Nine years ago to the very month, New Orleans was host to the General Conference of Negro Lutheran Churches. This was a Synodical Conference organization and, while it had almost as many white pastors as Negro pastors, it was still a segregated organization because the white pastors were pastors of Negro congregations. Here in New Orleans I was elected President of the General Conference and accepted, with the avowed intention of presiding at its funeral.

Our sessions were to end with a service to be held in the Municipal Auditorium. I was to be the speaker, the first Negro speaker ever to appear in the auditorium. This I was supposed to accept as an honor. A Negro pastor was to serve with me. He was scheduled to be the liturgist.

All arrangements for this service had been made by some of my local white colleagues. They explained that there would be white people at the service, but they would be seated in the balcony. When I expressed my opposition to this arrangement, one of them laughed and said that it might be a good thing. For once, white people would see how it feels to be relegated to the balcony.

It wasn't easy to get them to understand that segregation is segregation, no matter who seems to get the short end of the deal. But, in reality, were the white people being segregated, or were we still the goats?

I tried to explain it like this:

Suppose you take me to the swankiest restaurant in town; suppose you seat me at the finest table in the place; suppose the best waiters serve me peacock tongues, caviar and pink champagne. Suppose, now, that everyone else in the place withdrew to the kitchen to eat hot dogs and mustard . . .

because they didn't want to eat with a Negro! Although you might think that I was getting the long end of the deal, I would feel as humiliated as if I had been kicked out in the beginning. It is the rejection that hurts!

There was a similar element, I told them, in the arrangements they had made for the service at the auditorium. They seemed shocked when I said that I would rather preach from a soapbox on Saint Bernard Circle than appear before a segregated audience.

The Conference agreed with me. So my local colleagues set out to make different arrangements. When they returned they said that all was well. There would be so segregation.

Later, however, we discovered that no segregation in their terminology meant that white and Negro worshipers would be seated on the same level, but that white people would occupy the seats off the shoulder aisles, and Negroes, the seats off the center aisle!

But it was too late now to do anything about it. So we prepared for the service.

I arrived at the auditorium early. There was a sprinkling of white people on the shoulders and a sprinkling of Negroes in the center. I then sent a local layman to tell the ushers not to seat anybody. Just meet the people at the door, give them the printed order of service, and let them shift for themselves . . .

If the god whom some Southern white men have created in their own image were the one true God, he would have torn the Municipal Auditorium from its foundations and cast it into the midst of Lake Pontchartrain. For our audience was thoroughly mixed when the service began . . . and we had substituted a white pastor from Washington, D. C. to serve as liturgist for the Negro speaker from New York!

The old building was still standing! It was still being used!
Nothing, absolutely nothing had happened to it!

It was time for us to leave New Orleans, and we still
wanted to sail in a glass-bottomed boat over the waters of
Silver Springs.

We knew before we left New York City that the distance
from New Orleans to Silver Springs was more than we cared
to drive without a break. But surely, we thought, somewhere
along the way there must be a motel or tourist home that
accepts Negro guests. In New Orleans we would inquire.

We did inquire . . . but no one among our friends or relatives could help us. There were some who had made the trip,
but they had done it non-stop. My wife, the first to be sold
on the Silver Springs idea, was the first to give it up. She
suggested that we return home the way we came, because
along that route we now knew the Negro stopping places.
But wait—I said—I have a friend who does a lot of traveling . . .

I found my friend right where I had left him nine years
before—sitting in a swing on the gallery of his uptown home.

When we had sat in this swing before, it was late in the
evening. The street lamp, shining through the trees, made
crazy patterns on the mosquito screen. Someone turned into
the yard and walked hurriedly up the steps. It was a red-
faced man wearing an expensive tan suit and a wide-
brimmed panama hat.

"Howdy, Son!" he boomed as he pumped my friend's
hand with his right and slapped him on the shoulder with
his left.

"It's nice to see you again, Uncle John," my friend responded.

The big red man and I were introduced. And my friend

56

yelled through the open door, "Alice, Uncle John is here!"

Uncle John went in and we returned to the swing.

"My wife's uncle is quite a character," my friend said in a voice that was just above a whisper. "He is a big Texas cattle man. . . . Not even his wife and children know that he is a Negro. Did you notice that he walked to the house? When he is in the city he stays at a ritzy downtown hotel. For some reason he is very fond of Alice, and always comes to see her. But, afraid of being caught at it, he has his Negro chauffeur drop him off before the big white homes on the avenue. Then he walks two blocks through a side street to get here where we live."

I laughed at this and said, "You know, I have heard it said that as many as twenty thousand Negroes a year pass for white. I don't believe it, because there is no accurate way of estimating the number of Negroes who pass. Still, I am sure that there are many who do, either part-time, for occupational reasons, or full-time, for social reasons."

"I know," my friend said, "I have done it myself on occasion. . . . I used to think that Negroes who pass could do a lot of good for the Negro race in the South. You know, like spies behind the enemy's line. They could speak up for Negroes. They could encourage white people who believe in fair play but are too timid to do anything about it. I used to think that, but not anymore."

I didn't know exactly where he was headed, but I was interested and didn't want to stop him. I waited out his silence and he decided to go on.

"You know," he said, "I do a lot of traveling. Last year I was in Texas and decided to drive by Uncle John's place just to see what it looked like. Out of curiosity, I began talking to some Negroes who lived near there. I asked them whether they knew this big cattleman and what kind of man

57

he was. And do you know what? . . . Every damned one said that he was the biggest nigger hater in Texas!"

He waited for my reaction, and when he didn't see it coming, he added, "Guess he thinks he has to do that to keep anyone from suspecting him. . . . I wonder how many of the race-mongers in the South are Negroes themselves."

Well, I couldn't answer his question nine years ago, and he couldn't answer mine now. He had been to Silver Springs, but on the way he had stopped at a white motel . . .

My wife had anticipated my failure. When I got back to the house she and Ruby had mapped out a new route for our return trip. Our first stop would be Birmingham. The man in Atlanta had said that there was a Negro motel there . . .

Buddie had gone to work. Only my sister was home—and Junior—the day we left New Orleans. While we were loading the car, Clemmie and Junior were playfully fighting their goodbyes.

We were not in a hurry. Birmingham was only three hundred sixty-five miles away. It would be an easy day's drive.

The gas was very low when we left the house, but we decided to let it go until we reached the open highway. After we had fought our way through the heavy morning traffic, we settled down to enjoy the scenery.

Noticing a desolate stretch ahead, my wife said, "What about the gas!"

Shortly, a lonely gas sign appeared. I cut my speed, pulled into a small clamshell driveway, and stopped before the only pump on the place.

There was a little one-room shack standing in a clump of bushes. The dirty white paint on the clapboard walls was peeling away. The tar paper shingles were curling with age.

The dirty screen door had a hole in it big enough for a bat to fly through. And across the bottom there was a sign saying: WHITE ONLY.

When I saw the sign I muttered something unpleasant and pulled out to the highway.

My wife said, "But we must have gas!"

I swallowed my anger and backed up to the pump.

From my seat behind the wheel I couldn't see a single sign of life in the dirty little shack. But suddenly someone emerged from the clump of bushes. It was a skinny little woman in a dingy white dress. She wore an apron that was tied around her waist. Her narrow, gray eyes stared from beneath the shield of an old-fashioned bonnet. Her wrinkled face was as dirty as the dress she wore, and the dip-stick she held in her mouth dripped snuff juice into the creases of her chin.

Creeping beside her was a skinny, sad-eyed hound.

It is said that a man grows into the image of his ideal. These two had grown into the image of each other.

The little old woman looked at me and said, "Yas?"

Unscrewing the top of my gas tank, I answered, "Five gallons, please."

She inserted the nozzle and ran in the gas. I screwed the top back on and handed her a five-dollar bill. She began to fumble for change . . . She had difficulty counting it . . . Finally she got it right and I drove away.

With the exception of her "Yas?" and my "Five gallons, please," the entire transaction had taken place in absolute silence . . .

This was where our road turned left. Following Route 11, we would have to cross the long, level Pontchartrain Bridge . . .

It was a beautiful day. My wife and her sister were marveling over the bright blue sky and the fantastic formations of the low-hung, silver clouds. Passing Clemmie the binoculars from our front-seat carrier, I called attention to the sleek, new motorboats and the white sails in the distance.

We were reaching the end of the bridge. The sign said: SLIDELL. Soon we would re-enter Mississippi. I could still hear talk of clouds and boats and white sails near the horizon, but it sounded like voices in another room. My memory began groping for place names, and from the days of my early childhood, came up with Logtown and Pearl River, Gautier and Mandeville.

Some time in the long ago, somewhere in this area, where the white man's creed is purity of race, the son of a plantation owner raped a Negro girl . . . and my father was born. . . . Somewhere in this area my blue-eyed, auburn-haired mother was born . . . How she and her parents ever achieved the dubious distinction of living as Negroes, I have never been able to discover . . . Only in the United States could that have happened . . .

In Mississippi and Alabama we avoided roadside picnic tables. In fact, throughout our whole trip we never stopped at a roadside picnic area where white people were present. And it seemed as though the white tourists were giving us a wide berth, too. Only once did a white car stop at a picnic area while we were there. The car wore an Ontario tag. So perhaps the young couple with two small children didn't know any better. Perhaps they were just entering the South and hadn't heard that if a white woman is scared by a Negro man her next child will be born black! . . .

It was almost dark, and we had begun to feel uncomfortable. It was time to look for rest rooms again. We passed a number of fine places, but most of them had fancy lunchrooms attached, and a lot of pretty white ladies were around. We were afraid to try . . .

After a while we pulled into a station and stopped at the pump. A baby-faced Negro attendant came out. He was so fat and soft that with every step he seemed to be walking in all directions at the same time.

I asked, "May we use your rest room?"

He looked embarrassed and piped in a childish voice, "I'm sorry, Sir, but, you see, it's like this. They just started here, and they haven't built a colored rest room yet."

Birmingham wasn't far away . . . not too far. . . . We would wait.

When we crossed the city limits we began to ask directions. From stop to stop we were steered closer and closer. Finally, we saw it—the new Negro motel . . . It was beautiful. We pulled into the spacious courtyard and unloaded.

When we were settled for the night, I decided to go out to the lobby to talk to the clerk about our next day's route and the possibility of finding a Negro motel in Nashville. The young lady behind the counter was busy with another guest. So I walked over to a quiet corner and sank into an easy chair. It was getting late and, with the exception of the clerk and the guest to whom she was talking, I was alone.

Then, a thin, dark man walked in. He was wearing a white sport shirt and dark blue slacks. When he reached the center of the room he turned in a small circle, his eyes slowly taking in his surroundings. I was watching him, and he knew it. He pulled a pack of cigarettes from his shirt pocket, stuck one into his mouth, and walked over to me for a light.

"Are you a guest here?" he said.

"Yes, just for tonight," I answered, "we're leaving in the morning."

"Where are you from?" he continued.

"New York City. . . . And you?"

"Oh, I'm from Alabama. I belong down here."

Yes, he did belong down there. He had received his education there . . . He was traveling from there to there and was stopping with a friend in the city. This motel was new to him. When he heard about it this afternoon, he decided to drive around to see what it was like.

"Beautiful place they have here, isn't it?" he said.

I replied, "Yes, for both comfort and beauty it leaves nothing to be desired."

"Did you notice the neighborhood?" he said, as he dropped into the chair next to mine. "If this place were out on the highway with the other motels, it would be wonderful, but stuck away in this rundown community, you have to come inside to appreciate it. It's a damned shame, isn't it?"

What could I say? It was a shame. I could only nod in agreement.

"And then," he went on, "you have to look for it. But, thank God that here there is one for you to find. I'm glad to see it . . . But why should it be that way? A white man can take a motorcycle and drive from one end of the country to the other in greater comfort than you can with the finest car on the road. Why should it be that way? He can stop a hundred times a day to eat and drink and rest and take in whatever the country has to offer. And he can do it without fear of embarrassment. He never has to enter a place with his heart in his mouth. . . . But look at you! A Negro has to drive sometimes until his tongue hangs out and he is ready to wet his pants before he can find a place where it looks safe to stop. And the way these people fight to keep you out of their toilets, you'd think that every Negro in the country had chancres on his behind."

I flinched at the language, but I couldn't deny the truth

62

of what he was saying. Wasn't that why I was here, to seek information that might ease the anxiety of my next day's drive? This bony-faced man was nervous . . . intense . . . eager to talk on a problem that he had lived with all his life. To give his subject direction, I asked, "What do you think about integration?"

"Integration?" he replied. "You mean this school business?"

"Yes, I . . ."

"You can't think clearly about the integration of schools until you air the whole system of segregation we have here in the South. Everything is involved . . ."

"Do you think that integrated schools will work?" I asked.

"Work? Sure it will work if the white people want it to work and will work at making it work. It won't be easy. It might be easier for the little children than for the older ones. If the parents didn't infect their children with this disease they call prejudice, the little ones would take it in stride . . ."

"Do you think that the little Negro children will be able to keep up with their white schoolmates?" I asked.

"Yes," he said, "but that depends. That's why I said the whole rotten system is involved. Negroes are discriminated against in employment. That means low income. They are discriminated against in housing. That means slum quarters and poor home environment. Because their parents have been brought up half-educated or even ignorant, there is little home training. The most training some Negro children get is on how to keep in their place and avoid offending the white man. And that's a lesson they have to learn for dear life's sake. But let's take these little Negro children and put them with white schoolmates. The Negro children from slum areas will do as well as white children from slum areas. Only there won't be as many of the whites. The Negro children who come from homes where parents can help them with their work will do as well as white children whose parents can help them with their work. The few Negro children who come from better homes, with well-educated parents, will do as well as white children from similar homes . . ."

I tried to butt in, but there was no stopping him.

"Now wait. . . . With the older children, those in high school, it's going to be a lot more difficult. You'll have the same situation you have with the little ones, but they will have an additional curse to bear. They have lived—I should say endured—longer than the little ones. They have been conditioned. They are so torn and twisted by insult and humiliation that they walk in a fog of anxiety and uncertainty. Man, it will take a whole army of psychiatrists to straighten these poor kids out. And . . . as far as you and I are concerned, we're hopeless. After all these years of inhuman treatment, we'll never be able to respond to human situations like human beings. Poor dogs of the earth, our guts will burn and our food will stick in our throats until the day we die. . . . You see, integration will work in our schools, but it is going to require teachers with patience, a genuine love for children, and an iron-bound will to do the thing that is right."

"You say," I interjected, "that the whole Southern system of segregation is involved. I believe that you are right. I believe that the man in the street must be made aware of that— the postman, the police officer, the housewife in her kitchen, the newsboy on the street, the factory worker behind his machine. They must realize that a change must be made. They must be made to see the eternal rightness of dealing with human beings as human beings. Our present system has made democracy a joke and Christianity a laughingstock. Now, if a change is to be made, it must be, first, a change of heart. And at this point, it seems to me, the clergy comes in. I have seen churches by the hundreds here in the South. Catholic priests and Protestant ministers have the Southern white people sitting before them every Sunday morning. Couldn't they help? Couldn't they inspire the people by word and deed to strive for the glory that could be theirs if they really practiced the political and religious creeds that remain unfulfilled, but that they are yet reluctant to let go?"

"Look, friend," the little man said, "don't put your faith in clergymen. If they really wanted to do something, they could. But how many of them want to? Why, I once saw a preacher throw a rock at a Negro boy. With my own ears I heard him call that Negro boy a little black bastard. I heard someone say that the white preachers in the South have both their knees in the black man's belly, and the louder they pray, the deeper they sink their knees. I believe it came from a book. But that's it! Even the best of them meet in conferences and pass innocuous resolutions; but when they stand in their own pulpits on Sunday morning, they're dumb. They preach sermons about the forgiveness of sins, but they never say that treating Negroes like you would not want to be treated in a sin."

"But," I said, "if white clergyman did point out the evils of segregation, do you think it would help?"

"No!" he shot back, "not unless they were men enough to admit their own sins. . . . Nobody has any respect for the clergy—not as spiritual leaders. Everybody knows that as far as spirituality is concerned, they're just a bunch of sanctimonious hypocrites. Nobody really respects them. They respect them like a person respects the president of the bridge club. The preacher is just the president of the church club.

65

And the church is just another social organization where a certain little group of friends meet for a Sunday morning get-together. Why, in some congregations, they don't even take in all white people. They take in only *their* kind of white people."

"But still," I insisted, "the man in the pulpit has the ear of his people . . ."

"I know!" he said, "What good does it do? He says what the people want to hear. And even if he did preach against the evils of segregation, do you think it would do any good? I tell you, nobody respects the Church, not even the devout members who attend. Look! Suppose a preacher began hammering away at the evils of segregation. First thing, his members would tell him to preach the Gospel and let the race problem alone. If he didn't stop, they might ride his tail out of town. Does that sound like respect? If he kept it up and stuck to his pulpit, they still wouldn't pay any attention to him. Why? It's because the Church never has been bound by segregation laws. If the Church wanted to, the Church could have integrated its congregations, its schools, its Sunday schools, all the way down the line. That could have been done fifty years ago, a hundred years ago. But the clergy didn't tell the people to do it. Now, when they talk about it, the people say if segregation is an evil today, it was an evil fifty years ago. Why didn't you tell us then? If it wasn't evil then, why do you talk about it now? . . . And what can the preachers answer? . . . You can't respect that kind of clergy.

"If the Church of the South really wanted to help, it could. But, first, the preachers will have to be humble enough to repent of their previous cowardice, and men enough to tell the people that they were wrong. With that as a starting point, they may be able to gain the respect of their parishioners, and when that is done, the parishioners will listen.

"But watch what I tell you—some of the clergymen of the South are going to capitalize on the prejudices of their people. They are going to remind them that the Supreme Court desegregation decision does not apply to churches and church institutions. The result will be that we are going to have a rash of new church schools in the South. . . . Watch what I tell you."

I made a move to go, but it was no use. The little man was steaming.

"Look!" he said, reaching for another cigarette (now he had a lighter). "In a way, religion is all mixed up in this thing. The only real religion the Southern white man has is purity of race, and on that he is a religious fanatic. And that is not so ridiculous as it seems, for after all, race is a matter of faith. No man knows his race. . . . I don't care who you are, in the final analysis both you and your father have to take your mother's word for it."

He shifted his weight, stared into space and leaned toward me. Tapping my knee with a nervous forefinger, he said, "Do you want to get down to the heart of the matter? You know what it is? . . . It is the attitude of the Southern white man over against sex. It is an obsession, a sickness."

He paused a while, waiting for my reaction. With a nod of my head, I replied, "Possibly."

Taking this as his cue for elaboration, he said, "For generations the Southern white man has been living a lie. He has been preaching purity of race by day and going to bed with Negro women by night. But you can't do wrong and feel right. Sooner or later it gets you. So the white man has a guilty feeling over against Negro men. He feels that the Negro ought to want to repay in kind; and, afraid that he might, he makes an affair between a Negro man and a white woman a crime punishable by death—at least, for the Negro man.

"At the same time, the sex-mad white man has a guilty feeling over against his wife. To make amends, he kisses her reverently and stands her on a pedestal. Now, a fact that he will not face is this: in many cases, while he is out stalking Negro women, his wife slips from her pedestal and goes out to seduce Negro men. In both cases the white person is usually the aggressor. Especially is this true in the case of white women and Negro men. The Negro man has to be assured and reassured, because one yap out of the woman, be it from a simple lover's quarrel, or discovery by someone who might tell, and his goose is cooked. . . . It has always been so. . . . In most cases the woman was frightened into yelling 'Rape!' and the man was run down and. . . . You know the story. . . . It is only recently, very, very recently, that Negro men and the white women caught together have been dealt with in a manner that has any semblance of sanity.

"And, of course, there are cases in which white women simply moved into a strange community and passed for colored. There are others who escaped the South and went up North to live with their Negro lovers."

"Yes," I found myself joining in, "I have met some of them. I am thinking now of one I know. She is living in a Negro neighborhood with a Negro husband. But very few people notice it. For all they know, she is a light-skinned Negro. The truth is that she is a white woman from—of all places—Georgia!"

"Georgia!" The little man slapped himself on the knee. There was a dry cackle that was meant to be a laugh. "Man, if old 'Hummon' Talmage heard that, he'd kick the dirt out of his face and climb right out of his grave!"

68

He was quiet for a moment . . . grave. And then he said, "Don't let me lose track of my point—this sex religion of the Southern white man. Now, if the Southern preachers had the respect of their people . . . if they were accepted as spiritual leaders . . . and if they really wanted to, they could do a great deal of good."

"How so?" I asked.

"Wait, let me go on. . . . The preachers ought to go all-out against the law that forbids intermarriage. Instead of condoning this thing, they ought to tell the people that intermarriage is not a sin, but that adultery is. They ought to insist that if a white man and a Negro woman want each other, they must do it within the bonds of holy matrimony. They ought to insist that if a white woman and a Negro man want each other, they must come together honorably in sacred wedlock. And they ought to use their influence to help create a social atmosphere that will, on the one hand, welcome the sinless union of a mixed couple, and on the other, condemn the filth and dirt of clandestine affairs.

"If this is done, if adultery is branded as sin, and holy matrimony given its rightful place in the Southern scheme of things, there would be less crossing of the race line than we have today."

"I, too, am convinced," I said, "that the white man's concept of intermarriage is a very potent factor in human relations . . ."

"But what I am trying to get you to see," he said, "goes deeper than that. On this point the white man is sick, and radical treatment is indicated. In many places in the South, Negroes outnumber white people. For this reason the white man is deathly afraid to compete with Negroes on equal terms. He wants to keep his better home, his better job, his source of cheap labor, his political power, his means of satis-

69

fying his need to have someone to look down upon . . . He needs desperately to protect this sacred heritage. So what does he do? . . . By some diabolical alchemy his sick mind creates an image, a symbol of all his ill-got possessions. And this symbol is the Southern white woman. He places a halo over her head and drapes her figure with a snow-white veil. Then he turns to the Negro man and tells him that to look upon this holy thing is to die."

The little man was trembling. He settled back in his chair, took a deep breath, and then leaned forward again. "You see what I mean?" he asked. "For an obsession like this, radical treatment is necessary. Somebody has to tear away the veil and convince the sick white man that this thing he has created is only a woman. Somebody's got to be brutally blunt about it and state the truth just this simply:

"A black woman suckles her young; a white woman suckles her young. A black woman has a navel; a white woman has a navel. A black woman sits on her behind; a white woman sits on her behind. A black woman has her period once a month; a white woman has her period once a month. A black woman eats and has to go to the bathroom. A white woman eats and has to go to the bathroom. If a black woman doesn't wash, she stinks; if a white woman doesn't wash, she stinks. If you close your eyes and pinch their bottoms, you can't tell one from the other."

"The white man's symbol has got to be unmasked. He has to be told that women are all the same. Our boys back from overseas say it ain't so, what they say about Chinese women. All over the world a woman is a woman is a woman is a woman. . . . Somebody's got to tell the Southern white man that his home-made idol ain't no danged white goddess. . . . And that everybody knows it but him!"

His eyes ran over and splashed his clean white shirt. His

dark skin showed through the big, wet spots. "Don't think that I am trying to disparage Southern white women, or any white woman. Some of them are chaste and some of them are immoral; some of them are frigid and some of them are passionate; some of them are normal and some of them are deviates. But to say this is no disparagement. It simply means that they are women like all other women. And I doubt that any of them want to be anything more than that—just women!

"Why should I speak lightly of women? . . . I'm not speaking lightly of women. I'm speaking of this damned symbol that the white man has created—this thing for which he keeps his foot on the black man's neck.

"I couldn't disrespect a woman. . . . My mother was a woman . . . tall . . . and black . . . and she walked like a queen, even on the downtown streets. . . . But they pinched her tail, too, when she was working in the white folk's kitchen. . . . She thought I was asleep, but I wasn't. I heard her crying to a neighbor about it. What could she do—quit? . . . She had three small children and her old, sick mother to feed . . .

"But she did quit, though. . . . Not long after, she got a job with another family. Rich people. They had a son attending Duke. He came home for the Christmas holidays, and one day found Annie. (That's what we called my mother, like everybody else. We called my grandmother Mamma.) He found Annie making up a bed and jumped on her. She screamed, and his mother came running. At first the old lady was hysterical. By the time she got control of herself, the boy had left the house. . . . She fell down on her knees and buried her mixed-gray hair in Annie's lap and cried, 'Annie, don't say anything about this, please, Annie. . . . You have boys of your own, Annie. Someday this could happen to you. . . . Annie . . . you know what it means to be a mother . . .' You see, she knew what every white man has to know—that she was just a woman . . . a mother with a heart full of sorrow . . .

"You see, if clergymen were really men of God, they would be able to make people see these things. If these so-called ministers and priests and rabbis . . ."

"Listen," I interrupted, "are you a Communist?"

He looked hurt . . . really hurt.

He said, "Who are you? What do you do? That remark you just made is straight out of Dixie. Whenever a man says that Negroes are treated unfairly, they call him a Communist. . . . If a Negro says that he wants to be treated like a human being, and then a Communist comes along and says that the Negro ought to be treated like a human being, does that make the Negro a Communist? If a Negro says he wants his children to have a decent education and be able to live without fear, and a Communist comes along and says that this is not an unreasonable request, does that mean tha the Negro is following the Communist line?

"I know the Communists. . . . I know, too, that they tried their best to capture Negro America. But the American Negro wants to achieve human status by constitutional means, by democratic process. The Communists met their greatest failure among Negro men. And they failed in spite of the fact that they often baited the trap with the tails of their prettiest women. . . . I read that somewhere. . . . I wish that every white man who thinks that every black man wants to go to bed with a white woman would stop to think about that . . ."

My little man had mentioned rabbis, and this set me to thinking about the Jews. . . . The only Jews I know in New York City are men and women who are good, fair-minded

72

citizens. They have a fellow feeling for the oppressed Negro. And some of them work harder to keep Christian youth with Christian churches than many Christians do.

Somewhere on my shelves I still have an unbound copy of a book called *The Devil and the Jews*. When I read it some years ago, I was startled. The methods of persecution which the Christians used against the Jews were exactly like those used against Negroes today. These weapons have been sharpened by use. These techniques of torture have been developed in the course of centuries. And today the American white man has them down to a fine art. . . . I felt that the Jews and the Negroes had a lot in common.

"How do the Jews act down here?" I asked.

"The Jews? You mean how do they treat Negroes? Hell, they are as bad as the others. The only reason they don't belong to the Ku Klux Klan is that they would have to affirm their faith in Christ. . . . You see, to be a member of the Klan you have to be White, Protestant, Christian. The Klan, you know, whips and burns and kills in the name of Jesus. They instill fear by the sign of the Cross. They spread terror in the name of the Prince of Peace.

"Although the Jew may become a big man in business or politics, he is not quite accepted by the upper crust, the elite. The cream of Southern society is still White, Protestant, Christian. But things are looking up for the Jews. New hate groups are forming. They want to strangle the Negro economically. For this they need the help of the Jews, because they control a lot of money in the South. So, for once, the Jew can get into the inner circle. Now he has a chance to show that he can torture Negroes with the best of Christians, that he is truly worthy of complete acceptance."

The little man grabbed his stomach and grimaced in pain.

"What's the matter? Is something wrong?" I asked.

"No," he said, "nothing unusual. It's just the great American melting pot."

"The what?"

"The great American melting pot. Don't you know what it is? It's right here," slapping his stomach, "right here in the black man's belly. And the white man keeps it boiling. Every time it simmers down, he throws on another faggot of insult or injury . . .

"Look, I gotta go." He rose from his chair and said, "But what is your line? . . . You didn't tell me."

"You didn't give me a chance," I answered. "I am a minister."

"A min— I'm sorry." It came in a whisper. . . . He screwed his cigarette into the ash stand and hurried out. . . . My little black man was lost in the darkness.

Sorry? . . . But I wasn't sorry. This was grass roots reporting, and I found myself wishing that every clergyman in the country could have heard it. . . . Who was that big church official who said that Negroes would be satisfied with their lot if only the white agitators would let them alone? . . . How dumb can big men get? . . . None so blind as one who will not see . . .

The girl had left the counter and a man had taken her place. But he couldn't help me. He didn't know of a Negro motel in Nashville, Tennessee. I would have to take my chances . . .

After breakfast the waitress prepared our food for the day, filled our water jug . . . and we were off.

According to our map, we could have taken a more direct route to Nashville. But along almost every highway we had traveled we had seen rooftop signs saying: SEE LOOKOUT MOUNTAIN. It got to be a habit with Clemmie. Every

74

time he saw a sign he'd yell, "Let's go to Lookout Mountain!" It was only small talk. He knew that we did not intend to go there. We were headed for Silver Springs. But since our trip had taken an unexpected turn, we discovered that we could visit Lookout Mountain and still reach Nashville at a reasonable hour.

The weather was good that day, and driving a pleasure. I don't know how long we had been on the road when we saw the first one, but somewhere there was a sign saying: RUBY FALLS, and then other signs turned up with increasing frequency. It became a joke to Clemmie. He wanted to see where Aunt 'Ruby Fell.' The signs became so insistent that we all became curious and soon found ourselves following the arrows up a mountainside to Cavern Castle, the entrance to Ruby Falls.

We walked into a waiting room similar to that of a small town railway station. When we bought our tickets we were told that we would have about fifteen minutes to wait for the next elevator. So we milled about the room, not knowing whether to stand or sit. I had a feeling of being watched . . .

"You won't have long to wait," someone said.

The sound was pleasant, and when we turned we looked into a smiling face. It was the clerk behind the souvenir counter, a woman, middle-aged and attractive.

"We have a lot of people down there today," she said, "people from everywhere, even from India and Spain. We get them like that some days, people of every race and nationality."

Was she making talk . . . or had she read the trouble on my face? Did she understand the fear that haunts a Negro when he enters strange surroundings? It seemed so. . . . She was trying to make us feel at ease.

My wife, who always responds to a smile with a bigger

one, walked over to the counter, and soon she and the smiling lady were talking like childhood friends.

We bought several souvenirs of the place, and when the lady had wrapped them, she insisted on holding them for us.

"You will have a long walk when you get down to the cave," she said. "You will enjoy it better if you have no packages to carry . . . and don't forget to sign our register!"

It was too late to sign the register then. The elevator had come and it was time for us, and the twenty or twenty-five visitors who had come later, to go.

The elevator dropped us two hundred sixty feet. A guide was waiting there. He told us that occasionally we would have to stop and line up against the wall to let returning parties pass. On our return we would have the right of way.

Through narrow corridors of amazing splendor, past stalagmites and stalactites of solid onyx, we wended our way to a depth of over eleven hundred feet. Suddenly we found ourselves standing at a giant archway . . . and beyond was darkness.

The guide said, "We are now at Ruby Falls."

He turned on the light. We stepped through the archway into a stone rotunda, hewn by the hand of God. In the center there was a sparkling pool into which water was pouring from above. We lifted our eyes and followed this ribbon of water until we lost our breath. From one hundred forty-five feet above it came, pushing its way from a mountain crevice and leaping to the pool below, falling as it had been falling when the first boatload of Negroes landed on Virginia's shore . . . when the founding fathers said *men are created equal* . . . when the burdened slaves sang their plaintive melodies in the darkness of the night; falling as it had been falling when Lincoln said that black men should be free . . .

Now we understood the reverent silence of those returning from this scene . . .

While I was signing the register my wife went to pick up our packages. I joined her later, as the smiling lady was saying, "Have you seen our dining room? Since you have a long drive ahead, you will have to stop to eat somewhere. You might as well eat here. Just go in and take a seat anywhere you please. The girls will be happy to serve you."

Well, why not? This was the first time we had found an opportunity like this in the South. Why not make use of it?

The dining room was not a large one, but evidently large enough for the traffic. There were several tables vacant. We chose one and sat down.

Three girls in their late teens seemed to be in charge. They looked like high school girls working during their summer vacation. Two were black and one was white. The two black girls waited tables, while the white girl sat behind the cash register, going to town on a wad of gum. All three had on soiled white dresses. All three laughed and talked and kidded each other in a spirit of intimate friendship, like equals. In fact, the only concession to Southern tradition was that the white girl was handling the money. Otherwise, there was perfect equality—equality of dirt and grease and slow, sloppy speech.

After we had eaten we returned to the waiting room, and I began looking for the toilets. The man at the counter said that they were on the mezzanine. And they were. But over one of them there was a big sign saying: COLORED.

I thought of the little black man in Birmingham. Perhaps he was right . . .

Here white and black could sit together in the waiting room; they could visit Ruby Falls together in the bowels of the earth; they could eat together in the small dining room;

77

but they couldn't use the same toilet. . . . I'm sure, however, that she was not responsible for this arrangement . . . not the nice lady . . . the lady who smiled at us . . .

Rock City Gardens on Lookout Mountain is not very far by mountain road from Ruby Falls.

There were scores of tourists there when we arrived, men and women and children, laughing and talking, or just gazing with mouths wide open at the delightful, the awe-inspiring, the indescribable handiwork of old Mother Nature herself.

But among all these people there was no one who said Howdy—not to us, anyway. But that didn't hurt us any, that no one said Howdy. For under the circumstances, we felt that this was normal. These scores of people looked like one, big, happy group. But this was an illusion. Like us, all had come in carload groups, and the laughing and talking was, no doubt, within these carload groups. That was normal. So we did not feel hurt because no one had said Howdy. In fact, I don't know why I mention this, unless it is to say that we were satisfied that no one had said GIT!

After all, that is all we want—that men might let us be . . . let us walk God's earth like human beings and not invoke a penalty because our skins are black . . .

It was fun walking from Grand Corridor along the Enchanted Trail over Swing-Along Bridge and through Fat Man's Squeeze, where Clemmie said, "It's a good thing Aunt Kat is not with us. As fat as she is, we would have to turn around and go right back."

The thing that held Clemmie spellbound was Fairyland Caverns. Here, in God-made caverns, were many man-made wonders, tiny witches and goblins and princesses, illuminated by black light, all over the place. Here the Mother

78

Goose characters were brought to life, and Clemmie moved from one to another in wide-eyed wonder. In fact, we all enjoyed it. Perhaps it was . . . escape!

It was all a sight to remember. But the thing that I shall never forget was the lookout point over Lover's Leap. From this point one can look through high-powered binoculars into seven states.

That day the sky was blue, the air was clear, and there wasn't even a mountain haze to obstruct the view. The high-ways looked like ribbons draped across the hills, and auto-mobiles, like plastic models on the living room floor. Raising the glasses, I looked into Alabama, Georgia, South Carolina, Virginia, Kentucky, and Tennessee. From this high up, in all these Southern states, I couldn't see a single sign that said: FOR COLORED.

God! . . . forgive the thought . . . it isn't true, is it, that from where You are, You can't see them either?

We had spent a lot of time at Ruby Falls and Lookout Mountain. So it was late when we reached the outskirts of Nashville. On both sides of the highway the fancy, new motels were blazing in all their neon glory. . . . And we had to find a place to stay.

My wife is usually a very timid person, and she is rather apprehensive of long trips in an automobile. She is not yet quite convinced of their safety. For that reason she always gives the driver a lot of room and sees to it that nothing obstructs his view or hinders his movements. So what she did was the thing I least expected.

We were approaching a large motel that horseshoed into half a square. I cut my speed and began a turn into the driveway. Suddenly, my wife dived for the steering wheel,

79

and screeching, *"You can't go in there!"* tried to turn me back into the road.

Holding on for all I was worth, I kept my course and said, "I'm only going to ask for information."

"But you know they don't want you in there," she said. "I'm staying right here in the car."

I thought that Clemmie was still asleep in the back seat with his head on Ruby's lap. But as I was getting out of the car he yelled, "Daddy, may I go with you?"

"No, Clemmie!" his mother answered. "In fact, I don't like the idea of your daddy's going in there."

It looked like the lobby of a luxury hotel. There were plush seats and potted palms . . . and couples strolling around looking as though they had nothing to do but luxuriate.

The clerk was talking to two young women at the counter. When they turned to go, he looked my way, and I said, "I am looking for quarters for four."

The two young women turned back to ask another question of the clerk. When he had satisfied them, he turned to me again and said, "Where are you traveling?"

"From New Orleans . . . we're headed back to New York."

"How do you like this part of the country?"

"It's beautiful," I said. "A little hot, but on the whole, the weather has been fine for driving?"

Turning to look for vacancies, he said, "Let's see now, you want quarters for four. Can you use two double rooms?"

I repeated, "I need quarters for four," and added, "Negro tourists."

He dropped a key, turned quickly, and said, "But we couldn't house them here! . . . Wait, maybe I can find something."

He dialed a number, and asked over his shoulder, "Can you use two double rooms?"

"Yes, that will be sufficient," I answered.

He listened for a few minutes on the phone, taking notes.

"Look," he said, "this is what we have. This is a nice colored hotel. They can give you two rooms, both air conditioned."

Taking a folder from under the counter, he placed it on top and carefully traced my way on a small city map, explaining each turn I was to take.

None of the people strolling in and out had turned to look. . . . Perhaps they too had taken me for a sunburned white man. . . . I thanked the clerk and returned to the car . . .

A shirt-sleeved man led us up the stairs to the second floor. He showed us two rooms, each with a face bowl.

"Where is the bath?" I asked.

He replied, "That is down the hall. Come, I'll show it to you."

"But don't you have rooms with bath?" I asked.

"Let's see," he answered, "there may be one. Let me check on it. I'll be right back."

He returned and said that there was a room with bath on the same floor. We could have one with bath and one without.

The rugs were threadbare, the furniture cheap, the mattresses uneven. The walls were freshly painted. But what they needed was not new paint, but new walls.

Would it be any different, I thought if German-Americans had to have German hotels? If Italian-Americans had to have Italian hotels?

There are places in our country where there are only a

few German-Americans (or Italians, as the case may be). But even where there is a considerable number, they live and eat and sleep in their own homes in the community. Now, suppose German-Americans were not permitted to use the regular hotels. Suppose they had to find a German hotel—a German hotel, built and maintained only for an occasional German traveler, would be a business failure. There wouldn't be enough traffic to support it. So, in most cases the quarters would be poor and the service something one would rather do without. Waiting for an occasional German-American diner, the knockwurst would burn and the sauerkraut would stick to the bottom of the pot.

Instead of complaining about our accommodations, I sought out the owner and commended him.

After all, the rooms were air-conditioned. So, on a hot night in July, we fell asleep . . .

The next morning, when we had prepared for the day we checked out of the hotel. Our first stop was at Meharry Medical College, the Alma Mater of probably half the Negro doctors in the United States. For decades, most of our Negro doctors have been trained either here at Meharry, or at Howard University in Washington, D. C. Other institutions either excluded Negroes altogether, or kept their numbers down to a bare token admission by a vicious quota system. Many of the graduates of this institution represent some of the nation's unsung heroes, men who trained against great odds, practiced under almost unbelievable conditions, and did more for our country's health than the average man will ever know.

Next, we toured the campus of Fisk University and stopped for a visit to Jubilee Hall. This is the home of the world-famous Fisk Jubilee Singers, a group of skilled musicians whose performances created the myth that Negroes are born singers. To this day there are white people who believe that any Negro can sing. Even I, a tone-deaf foghorn, have been asked to sing!

I wonder why so many white people persist in believing this—that Negroes are natural singers. Of course, to admit that Negro singers had to be trained to sing, would be to admit that they had the ability to learn. To admit that they have the ability to learn, is to admit that they have a certain amount of intelligence. And this is an admission that some white people seem unwilling to make. For some reason, they prefer thinking of outstanding Negro singers as natural singers, and to them, Negroes who have achieved excellence in any other field are freaks!

At State College we found Carl in the office. Mary was in class. But soon a bell rang and Mary joined us.

Carl had turned gray, and it was becoming. Mary was ten years older than when we saw her last, but you wouldn't have guessed it. She was as pretty as ever.

It was good, seeing them again!

There was talk of Doris and her husband and of Clemmie and what a big boy he was. There was talk of Lydia and Doctor Thaxton and what became of the Dents. . . . But nothing was said about the Church. . . . There was talk of President Bluford at Agricultural and Technical College, and Doctor Jones at Bennett. There was talk of Greensboro and Atlanta, New Orleans and Birmingham. . . . But nothing was said about the Church. . . . That is, not until Ruby and Clemmie and Glenice and Mary were saying goodbye. Then Carl pulled me aside . . . and taking my hand in both of his, he said, "In spite of everything, Clem, Mary and I are still grateful to you and Glenice for reviving our interest in the Church . . ."

When I was getting into the car, Clemmie said, "What's the matter, Daddy? Did something get into your eyes?"

My sunglasses soon hid the something in my eyes. . . . But there was still something in my heart . . .

We rolled off the campus into the street and sought the open road . . .

When I was pastor of a church in Greensboro, North Carolina, Carl was teaching chemistry at Agricultural and Technical College in the same city. Mary was teaching chemistry in another local school. Carl and Mary and their daughter Doris attended our services and eventually fell in love with our simple liturgy and simple message of sin and grace—the simple story of Calvary's Cross. One day this little family was confirmed. I shall never forget their kneeling at God's altar to pledge undying allegiance to their God . . . and to the Lutheran Church. . . . To say that we were all very happy about it is to put it mildly.

Carl became active in our work with the boys of the parish. Later he was elected treasurer of the congregation. A popular figure in the community, he was often called upon to serve as speaker at various community affairs. He was the kind of person who would be an asset to any congregation.

Shortly after I accepted a call to New York City, Carl accepted a position as head of the Department of Chemistry at the State College in Nashville, Tennessee. Mary accepted a position, under Carl, in the same department.

After Carl had settled in Nashville, he decided to look up his Church—the Lutheran Church. The only thing he could find, however, was a white Lutheran church. And there he was told that he and his family would be permitted to attend the services, but that they would have to use a rear entrance and sit in a little room off the chancel. From this convenient hiding place they would be able to see the pastor at the altar and hear the services.

As these things came to mind, my melting pot, that had been simmering all the morning, began to boil.

What difference did it make to this Cornell Ph.D. that many of the members of that church were not his social and intellectual equals? . . . He was not seeking fellow scientists with whom to study, but fellow saints with whom to worship. Denied the communion of saints in his own household of faith, Carl and his family joined a Presbyterian church. . . . Thank God for the Presbyterians!

God, don't let me get sick on this trip. . . . Quiet my stomach . . . ease the pain . . . let me hold out until I get back home . . . and, Lord, this . . . this whole sickening mess . . .

Heavenly Father, wilt Thou not speak? . . . How long shall the flaming cross be a thing to dread and Thy blest Name a thing by which men curse? . . . Don't let this last, best hope of men succumb, and earth be damned by a hammer and sickle. . . . Must Thine own salt of this earth be salt that's lost its savor? . . . Must Thine own light of this world be light that failed? . . . Surely, there must be seven thousand in Thy many pulpits who have not bowed their knees to Baal. . . . Hast Thou not placed them there for such a time as this? . . . Must they forever cringe and cry and sob with inward pain: "The good I would, I do not; the evil that I would not, that I do?" . . . Must they forever cringe before the howling mob? . . . Must they forever sleep their fitful sleep and hide their eyes from facts of day? . . . Dear God, open up their mouths . . . let Thy Holy Spirit take some pointed word from Thy Holy Book and stab them wide awake. . . . *Let the righteous speak!* . . . Let the sons of God stand up and be counted! . . . If no courage comes from

Thee, dear God, these poor souls are going to stew in their own juice . . .

On this trip the seventh President of the United States became an old friend of ours. In North Carolina we passed a place where he had practiced law. In New Orleans we saw him astride his horse in Jackson's Square, and found many reminders of his colorful career in the Cabildo. Now the sign ahead was saying: HERMITAGE. This was the Tennessee home of the famous hero of the Battle of New Orleans.

We must have spent an hour at the Hermitage. In the museum, Clemmie planted himself before the swords and guns and cannon balls. We dug him up and moved on to the carriage house. In Jackson's home we walked through the corridors from room to room, trying to visualize what his home life must have been. In the garden we met someone who told us tales of Uncle Alfred, the General's Negro body-servant. And then we visited Uncle Alfred's house behind the big house and Uncle Alfred's grave behind the big grave . . .

We pulled into the highway and turned the car toward the Blue Ridge Mountains.

It was cool that evening, and we rolled the windows against the mountain air. Clemmie began swallowing hard and pounding his ears with his palms. He said that he had an attack of "the altitudes." Eventually he became accustomed to the elevation and his "altitudes" passed away.

We didn't waste any time on the road that day. My wife doesn't like mountain roads even in daylight, and after dark she becomes uneasy. I was glad that the worst was over at nightfall.

As we approached Asheville, Clemmie began reading the

motel signs: NO VACANCY . . . NO VACANCY . . . NO VACANCY.

Suddenly he said, "Look, Daddy! There's one. The sign says, 'VACANCY!' "

In a voice that bristled with irritation, his mother said, "Clemmie, by now you ought to know that we can't stop there!"

After a moment of silence, Clemmie answered, "I know, Mamma. . . . Come on, Daddy, let's go look for a flea bag . . ."

But it wasn't necessary to look for a flea bag. I knew where I was going—or thought I did. I was driving from memory. After correcting one false turn, we pulled up at THE RABBIT TOURIST COURT.

Two summers ago we had stopped at this place. We had come up to see the famous outdoor drama, called *Unto These Hills.* Clemmie was with us that time, too . . . and Ruby and Elva. When we drew up before the neon rabbit racing across the sign, someone read: RABBIT TOURIST COURT FOR COLORED. Everyone got out of the car but Clemmie. Thinking that he was asleep, I reached in to pick him up and carry him. But his eyes were wide open. There was a look of distress on his face. He whispered, "Daddy . . . is everyone in this car colored?"

Something happened to my heart. . . . "Yes, Clemmie," I said, "we may go in here. . . . We are all colored."

My little boy was wide awake. He could have walked. But I carried him in . . . and held him close . . . and prayed that somehow God would let him understand and . . . without bitterness . . .

The next day we fairly rolled down the mountainside. We stopped for a few minutes to look at Chimney Rock through our binoculars, and then it was King's Mountain, Charlotte, Salisbury, Winston-Salem.

We spent the night with Elva and the next evening found us home in Petersburg.

It felt good to be back home again. My vacation was not quite over. I still had a few days to relax before returning to the grind of Manhattan . . .

Clemmie was coming through the white lattice fence that separates our back yard from Vergie's. He had been watching several boys swimming in Vergie's pool.

Eddie turned in the front gate and ran back up the drive way. Eddie is a black-haired white boy who lives in Cleveland. He was visiting relatives who lived down the street.

Before long, Peter came in. Peter lives several blocks away. He had been helping his tall, black, unmarried aunt roll her blonde, blue-eyed baby—one she found (according to the neighbors)—when she was called in to nurse a sick white man in the absence of his estranged wife.

For hours on end they played together, little black Peter, little white Eddie, and little tan Clemmie, three boys . . . being boys.

They had just run down the driveway and landed on the sidewalk when Julie came out. She slammed her front door several houses away, flew down the steps, and stopped at the picket fence.

Julie doesn't look like her father. He is skinny and stooped and eagle-faced, an animated cartoon of a back-country sheriff. He is the one who told a neighbor, when he heard that a Negro physician was attending her, that he would rather die than have a nigger doctor work on him.

Julie is not like her father. At least, she doesn't look like him. With her red shoulder bob flying in the wind, she rode the gate until the hinges screamed. Then she stopped and watched the boys, little black Peter, little white Eddie, and little tan Clemmie. Suddenly she shot across the street and yelled, "E-D-D-I-E! Come on over here and play. This playground is for white people."

Eddie stuck his hands into his pockets and walked slowly toward his house. Peter turned in the opposite direction and ran away. Clemmie kicked the gate open and walked slowly, ever so slowly, up the steps and across the porch. He turned to look toward Eddie's house, then, over his shoulder, at Julie. Snatching the screen door open, he ran through the hall and found his mother standing at the kitchen sink. His big eyes were swimming as they looked up from his sweaty face. He said, "Mamma, is Eddie white, too?"

> *O almighty God, merciful Father, I, a poor miserable sinner, confess unto Thee all my sins and iniquities with which I have ever offended Thee....*
> *I am heartily sorry for them....*
> *I pray Thee, of Thy boundless mercy ... forgive ...*